WHY SIBERIA?

WHY SIBERIA?

David G Hathaway

EuroVision Publications
Dewsbury Yorkshire

British Library Cataloguing in Publication Data:
A catalogue record for this book is available from the British Library.

ISBN 0-9525132-0-X

Note: 'EuroVision', referred to in the text, and introduced in the end
papers of this book, is the short name of Eurovision Mission to Europe, a
registered charity, of 75 Moorlands Road, Dewsbury, West Yorkshire
WF13 2LF. This book is published with the cooperation of Eurovision
Mission to Europe, through which David Hathaway organised much of the
work described in these pages.

Published by EuroVision Publications,
85 High Street, Thornhill, Dewsbury, West Yorkshire WF12 0PT.

Printed in Great Britain by Newsomeprinters Limited,
Smithies Moor Rise, Batley, West Yorkshire WF17 8AU.

Dedication

I dedicate this book to
the people of Russia
for whom Christ died and
for whom I give my life,
to demonstrate His love
for them and
my love for Him.

CONTENTS

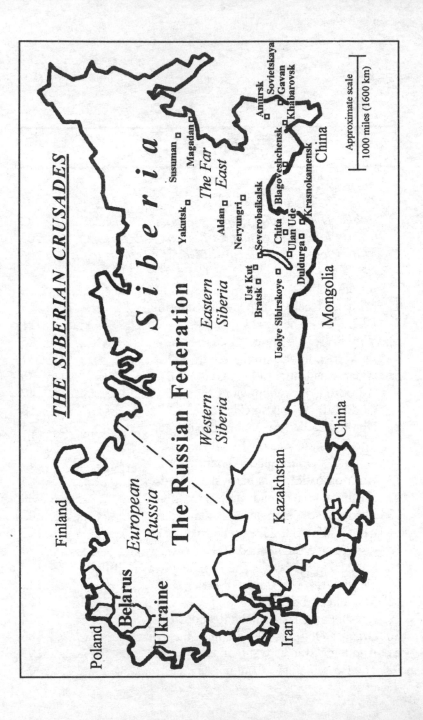

THE SIBERIAN CRUSADES

Finland

European Russia

The Russian Federation

Western Siberia

S i b e r i a

Eastern Siberia

The Far East

Susuman

Magadan

Yakutsk

Aldan

Neryungri

Severobaikalsk

Ust Kut
Bratsk

Usolye Sibirskoye

Chita

Ulan Ude

Duldurga

Krasnokamensk

Blagoveshchensk

Amursk

Sovietskaya

Gavan

Khabarovsk

China

Mongolia

Kazakhstan

China

Iran

Poland

Belarus

Ukraine

Approximate scale
1000 miles (1600 km)

Introduction

WHY DID GOD WORK SO MANY MIRACLES IN SIBERIA?

Seeing the hardships and difficulties, why did I go to Siberia? Why will I go again?

I receive no salary for my work with EuroVision as Evangelist, because my wife and I are trustees of the mission. No salary and no state benefits, I would be better off staying at home.

So much is said today about sowing into the mission field or Christian work in general - sowing finance into the work of God for the giver to receive financial rewards. I sow, not to receive finance but for two reasons: firstly because I love the Lord so much, secondly because my harvest is not finance but to see the glory of God in miracles, healings and souls won into His Kingdom. I believe in tithing but probably go further than most; I give Him the lot then let Him give me enough back to live on. The result is that I lack nothing and do not live in poverty!

So why did I go? Well, the Lord gave me a prophecy; a burning vision; and He spoke personally to me through His Word.

Every time I have had a major crisis in my life, God has dealt with me in the same way, offering me two alternatives. When I had the cancer in my throat all those years ago, I prayed and asked for healing. The answer was simple, "Trust Me, I will be with you and not forsake you; have the operation and even if you lose your voice, I will still provide for you - OR you can choose the hard way.'' Asking what that was He replied, "If you can pay the price, I will work a miracle and heal you." My answer was quick, "I want the miracle, whatever the price." The result was an outstanding miracle of healing that amazed the doctors and led me on the path that would eventually take me to Siberia. It was the same when I was in the prison in Czechoslovakia, desperate for my release. Despite much prayer, I was sentenced to a term of two years plus the threat of another five. I prayed so much and the Lord comforted me, telling me not to be afraid, that however long the sentence, however difficult the conditions in the prison, He would never leave me, He would support and sustain me, through hunger, torture and suffering. But again came the simple challenge - "OR you can choose the hard way. If you can pay the price, you can have your miracle and come out." I chose the hard way and God gave such a powerful miracle, showing me the exact day of my release, then using the British Prime Minister Harold Wilson to perform it.

With the vision for Siberia came so many promises. Having worked for over 30 years for Russia and Eastern Europe God had tested my faith to the extreme. In 1986 He gave me the vision that the Iron Curtain would fall. However in giving me the vision and prophecy, He also challenged me to fulfil it. The vision was to bring together believers from the East and West in a great conference in Karlsruhe in West Germany. When I shared this vision with some of the leaders, they did not believe me. I was left almost alone, but God had challenged me to fulfil it. So without any financial backing, I called the first East-West Conference in Karlsruhe for August 1988. God honoured His Word and 4,000 believers came together including over 600 from the whole of Eastern Europe and Russia. God then said to me, "This is not the end but the beginning," so I continued. This was to lead me into Bulgaria and Hungary in particular, then to the Ukraine.

After this I was fasting and praying about where to go next. Like David of old who used to ask God, "Do I fight these Philistines?" then afterwards, "If I fight will I win?" I began to ask Him for the strategy. God gave me 2 Samuel 5:17-25, where David enquired of the Lord and was told to attack the Philistines who were in Rephaim, and in verse 20 he defeated them. However two verses later they came against him again from the same place, Rephaim. So David again enquired of the Lord and was told not to attack from the front, but to go behind, wait until he heard the sound of marching in the mulberry trees, then attack them from the rear. The Lord said to me clearly, "This time go to the East of Russia, as far as you can, then wait for the sign, then attack." This of course was Siberia and the Far East.

Then He showed me prophecy from Deuteronomy 4:32-34 that He would do something so powerful in Siberia that the eyes of the whole world would be turned to see and marvel. So great would be the signs and wonders, that literally God says that we can ask from the beginning of time till now and from one side of Heaven to the other, from the East to the West, "Has God ever done such a great thing as this thing is?" What is about to happen would be the greatest demonstration of God's power in all of history and it would be in Siberia!

I asked Him, "How can I do it? No one will listen, they will not believe me and in any case how can I win the whole of Russia?" His answer was to show me Moses from Exodus 4:1 where Moses asks the same questions and God answers that it would be by the signs and miracles, which is exactly what this book will demonstrate.

When I asked Him, "What if no one will join me, what if there is not enough money?", He gave me 1 Chronicles 29, where David gives Solomon his son all the gold and silver, the materials and the men to build the Temple. For months I had seen myself as David and did not get the picture until the Lord indicated that He was like David in this context and that I was Solomon. His promise was that He would give me the men, the money and the materials.

When I fainted at the enormity of the task, He gave me 1 Chronicles 28:20, "Be strong and of good courage, and **DO IT!**"

In 1994 we did it. Now in 1995 we will go back for an even bigger project in Siberia. God has already said from Joshua 13:1, "There remains yet very much land to be possessed."

It amazes me because He showed me the whole of Satan's strategy for Russia, over a 700 year period from the rise of Genghis Khan until now, then showed me by vision and prophecy His plan and strategy for the salvation of Russia.

I have made a commitment to God and to the Russian people - my life for Russia - ALL of it, and I will only live on what He gives me back.

David G Hathaway

Chapter 1

MIRACLES REALLY HAPPENED IN SIBERIA

Our arrival in Khabarovsk was a nightmare of reality. From high up in the evening sunshine we had seen the clouds below us building up for a storm of tropical magnitude. As we landed the airport runway was like a lake, and we found that here in Siberia no airport staff came to help us. The fifteen of us had to unload everything ourselves. The men manhandled the heavy loudspeakers, amplifiers, baggage and all the other equipment out of the cargo bay and carried everything piece by piece across the flooded tarmac in the torrential rain and into the steamy arrival area. It was with a great sense of relief that we finally met up with the Pastor of the local church who had been alerted to come and meet us. He helped us pile everything into a waiting truck and ourselves into a car and mini-bus, then took us to where we were to spend the night, or rather what was left of it. I ended in some style in a private apartment with a warm welcome, but most of the team found themselves in total blackout, no lights because of the storm. They spent the hours of darkness either huddled two to a bed or on the floor without even the possibility of undressing, not even a cup of tea! The mosquitoes were the only ones who had any enjoyment that night!

We had started early that morning, the Siberian sun streaming through the window of the small rough room where I had slept, surrounded by boxes and papers, hardly an inch to move, my luggage pushed against the narrow bed, no space to unpack anything. No clean sheets, others had slept there before me, but I was very tired and had asked no questions the night before when I had arrived. Still there was a real excitement in the air as I climbed out of the bed and into my clothes.

Yesterday we had negotiated our first charter flight. Now in the early light of morning I saw the truck ready outside piled high with the sound equipment and music instruments. The fifteen of us tried to crowd into too few vehicles. Then another car came and I climbed in as we set off expectantly to the airport where the forty-eight seater AN 24, a Russian built Antonov turbo prop. airplane, would be waiting to take us the 2,200 kilometres on the last part of this journey to the third of our Evangelistic Crusades in Siberia.

We had not been able to obtain tickets on a normal scheduled flight from Ulan Ude to Khabarovsk, so we had needed to charter an airplane. The main airport at Ulan Ude had quoted a price of $10,000 for the five hour flight. However a businessman, not a believer, but so very helpful, offered us the charter of an identical aircraft from a smaller nearby private airport for only $4,500, less than half the price - and of course I had very willingly agreed!

Now as I waited with the team in the warm sunshine at 7.30 in the morning, all I had to do was sign the contract, pay over the cash in U.S. dollars and board the plane. We were due to take off at 8.00. As I sat on that chair in the upstairs office I wondered why it was taking so long, and why didn't these businessmen take my money? Then to my horror my new friend Thomas told me through my interpreter that the air-traffic control at the main airport were refusing us permission to take off, saying that if we attempted to do so we would be immediately shot down, either by Russian MIG fighters or by the military on the ground because, they said, we were in a sensitive area close to the Russian - Mongolian border.

The real problem, we discovered, was that this smaller private airport was undercutting the prices quoted by the state controlled airport, who in turn controlled the airspace. It was an absolute impasse. It could mean waiting days for them to resolve the situation, but more probably meant no flights at all, so I called the intercessors who were such a necessary part of our central team, to prayer. I too wrestled with God. I knew He had called us and we go by trust in Him. I received strong confirmation and confidence in my heart that God had spoken and that I personally had power with Him and would prevail, not only now, but throughout the whole of Siberia.

Soon after, our businessman friend Thomas emerged from the office to say that there WAS one way to solve the problem of getting airborne today - a direct personal appeal because of the nature of our work. He took us at high speed in his car to the main airport. He went in to talk to the directors, leaving us again to pray. Thirty minutes later we had his answer, OK we can fly, he had persuaded them to let us go! But as the car I was travelling in took a devious route back to the small airport I discovered another difficulty, our pilots had been sent home hours ago since the flight had been cancelled, and now we would have to locate them and get them back to the airfield. Calling at the home of the first we found that he had gone fishing, and the second pilot was not available either. We needed another miracle - we had permission to fly but no pilots!

Eventually by 2.30 pm local time, we had permission to load all the equipment onto the aircraft. It was getting late and we were hungry, having eaten little for breakfast, so Thomas bought us some bread and sausage to have on the flight. By now the missing pilots had been located, and the airport director came and asked me to sign the contract which would confirm the charter. I paid over the dollars and waited anxiously in the aircraft until at last we heard the soon to become familiar sound of the engines being started, and to our relief the plane taxied to the end of the runway. The engines vibrated urgently as the plane picked up speed, then as we became airborne our shouts of hallelujah and praise to God filled the cabin!

At last our lovely air hostesses , our praise and worship team, could begin to serve us our simple picnic lunch. Gallya, Elena and Asya had worked with me already for three years in the Ukraine. Being members of Pastor Anatoli's church in Kiev, they had assisted in leading the praise and worship in every crusade and conference which I had held in Kiev since 1991. Now Anatoli had really blessed me by sending them with the full support of his church to help me through this whole nine week period in Siberia. They are wonderful girls, strong spiritually and an essential part of our whole ministry, together with Roma who has just joined them.

This was the first time that we had flown in our own chartered airplane and it was a wonderful experience. Unfortunately we were to see how the devil would try to ruin even God's miraculous provision. Because of all the delays plus the fact that between Ulan Ude and Khabarovsk we would cross two time zones and so lose two hours, we arrived too late for the Crusade meeting, which was taken instead by the members of our waiting ground team. Jeremy Childs, who has been part of the EuroVision ministry for some years, preached the Gospel with enthusiasm. Many people who came found Christ, and many were healed, but of course we could not accurately record this meeting.

Now the memories of our long journey and traumatic arrival were behind us. Yesterday's storm had completely blown over. The Crusade on the Saturday night saw us under a powerful anointing of the Holy Spirit, and many hundreds crowded into the open-air of the football stadium as the praise and worship team ministered. Then when I made the appeal almost every person came forward, so many, that surely every one who had come into that stadium, lonely, lost, without faith or hope, and without Christ, found Him that night. Their hopelessness and despair had changed into the glory of the reality of knowing Him who loved us with a dying and undying love.

Then I said to them,

Here in Siberia, in the Far east of Russia, you have been taught for seventy years that there is no God, that He is dead. I can demonstrate, I can prove that He is alive. Look, I have no power of myself to heal the sick and crippled. If there is no living God, if Jesus is dead then tonight when I lay my hands on the sick no one will be healed or delivered. But IF God is alive then by the power of His Name miracles, signs and wonders will suddenly happen and this place will come alive with the power of God. But ONLY if Jesus is alive! THIS is the demonstration and proof!

I want to pray for the sick so that you can know God loves you and that He is concerned about the value of the human soul. Some people say Stalin killed as many as 100 million people, most of them died out here in Siberia. The fact is, if Stalin, from the first moment of his birth, had begun to write down the name of every individual who was to die under his regime, he would not have completed that list by the day he died. Under a system like this, people as individuals don't count.

But I want to tell you about a loving heavenly Father who puts such tremendous value on a human soul that He was willing His own Son should die just for you. This is the greatest revelation of all time, that God could love with such feeling and emotion, to set you free from sickness, sin and death to give you a freedom you've never understood. To know Christ is the only way to life. It's the living Christ who's alive today who can work miracles.

I want to tell you about a lovely fifteen year old Russian girl called Marsha who has just given her life to Christ. She said to me, "We've all done so much wrong. How is it then God loves us so much?" I wish I could answer that question. How CAN He love us that much? Even I don't know the answer, how or why - but I know He DOES love us. He IS concerned about us - He knows us, where we are, what we're doing, and He cares for us.

One reason I'm here is very special - it's because I KNOW how much God loves me. To have God as Father, to know the real love of God in my heart and life, to know He loves me enough to forgive every sin and heal every sickness - to have this kind of relationship with God is so wonderful, and I want YOU to have a relationship like this. God will forgive all your mistakes, all your problems, heal all your sickness - THERE IS NO LIMIT TO WHAT GOD WILL DO TO DEMONSTRATE HIS LOVE FOR YOU. If only you would turn to Him and ask Him for help. WHOEVER will call on Him, He WILL answer.

When I began to pray with the sick and crippled, the miracles which God had promised, began. A young man in a blue tracksuit moved forward patiently, showing no sign of the pain he felt or the desperation of his cry as a man to be made whole. His right hand had been crippled by a car accident. The doctors could do no more, their work had spared his hand but left it clenched and lifeless. BUT GOD..! I touched him, rebuking the cruelty and power of Satan, taking the strength and authority I have in Christ. In His Name I straightened those crippled fingers and brought back life and strength into that wasted hand. The joy and happiness which showed in his face as he began to move the fingers once dead! His thumb took a little longer, but it too responded to the Master's touch. Although it was collapsed rigidly into the palm of his hand, it finally came free and he knew Who had touched him.

We saw many exciting healings on the two days of the crusade I held in Khabarovsk. There was another man, middle-aged, also with a paralysed right hand from a car accident who was completely healed. A little boy with a greenstick fracture which he had had for one month and a ten year old girl with a deformity in her spine that made her left shoulder higher than the right were both healed. A middle-aged woman, whose fingers had been paralysed for a year after cutting her hand accidentally, was able to move and use them again. A fifteen year old girl was set free from pain in her spine which she had had since birth; then her mother, who had fallen and broken her back when she was only seventeen years old and for twenty years had suffered severe pain all over her body - in her back, shoulders, arms, hands, legs, feet -was instantly healed. A little boy was healed of a broken right arm that had set in the wrong position and another little boy, deaf after an operation, could hear again. A young woman was delivered from a curse spoken over her which had resulted in continual ringing in her ears. A mother brought her two young sons - the elder son overcame a speech impediment, and the younger son was healed of a hernia. On the last day an old woman pushed through the crowd to testify that the lump she had had on her knee the day before when I prayed, had gone and she was totally free of the pain. Cataracts dissolved, the blind saw, the arthritic were healed, the deaf heard - there were so many healings great and small!

I prayed for a two year old girl called Anya. She was dressed in a pretty pink frock and looked across at me shyly from the safety of her mother's arms. She held up her tiny fist with its lifeless thumb, paralysed from birth. She was due for an operation, but when she found she could wiggle it, she leaned over towards me and gave me a very bold and satisfied kiss! Another story that gives me joy to remember is that of eleven year old Vladimir. At the opening of the Sunday evening meeting, his mother took hold of one of our ushers to say that her son had been healed of near blindness the day before and had gone home so excited about this

Jesus and His power to heal, that he had persuaded her and all the apartment block to come along to the stadium and see for themselves what God can do. Vladimir himself later pushed his way through towards me to witness to his healing and to thank God.

There is one other rather curious story which moves me and which I shall always remember. A deaf man and woman - husband and wife - came together for healing. They were full of hope but also uncertainty. There was such pleading in their silent eyes. But they were not healed, not even with persistent prayer. Then I saw a lump on the woman's right wrist and, desiring so much to give her something that would build their faith, I placed my hand on hers. Immediately the lump and the pain vanished. She and her husband were lit up with wonder and amazement. I told them, through the little lad who was using sign language, ''The God who healed you of that lump is the same God who will also heal you of your deafness!''

Chapter 2

ULAN UDE - THE FIRST CRUSADE

Our first Crusade in Siberia shortly before had been in Ulan Ude which had also unexpectedly become our base camp. Originally we were to have used Chita as a base, partly because it is the principal airport for the whole region, but also because our main organiser, Misha, is Co-pastor of a very large and successful church there, and we needed to liaise with him as much as possible throughout the whole period of summer crusades. Unfortunately, long after our original plans were made, and only very shortly before we were due to put them into operation, a decision was made by the airport authorities to take advantage of the brief Siberian summer to completely re-surface the runways at Chita. This meant that no jets could land, only smaller propeller aircraft, virtually on a commuter basis.

Most of the central team had therefore arrived direct into Ulan Ude with me the day before our season of Siberian crusades was to begin. It had been a very tiring journey. We had flown into Moscow, some via Paris, some via Amsterdam, but with all the new restrictions in the Aeroflot timetable, none of us could make the onward connection to Ulan Ude the same day, so had had to spend the night in the International Airport as best as we could, some sleeping on chairs, others on the floor. The astronomical cost of a hotel was out of the question. The following day friends all the way from Kiev had organised to come and take the whole group by private bus to Domodedovo, the domestic airport, a drive of one and a half hours round the Moscow ring road.

So our arrival after the forty hour journey from England had left us tired but full of expectation for the first Crusade and we were not disappointed. The ground team who had arrived in Ulan Ude a week before under the leadership of Richard Wood, had done a good job. Their responsibility was to do seven days of street evangelism to prepare the way for the main Crusade. They had had a wonderful time, preaching and winning souls on the streets, distributing the flyers advertising the meetings and handing out tracts, in addition to sticking up the eye-catching posters, which announced the Jesus Festival. The result was that great crowds came to the football stadium. When I spoke the Word of God and called on those who would receive Him to come forward, the sight of those hundreds streaming down and emptying the stands was to make all the tiredness and hard work of the past months worthwhile. After I had prayed with the new converts, and the counsellors from the local churches had counselled them, we began the awesome task of praying individually as I always do with all the sick and crippled. Our God is wonderful at confirming His Word and fulfilling every promise. We saw so many of those desperately sick and hurting people healed and set free by the power of God.

Nearly one hundred claimed to have been healed when I showed them how to lay their own hands on their sicknesses and call upon the Name of the Lord. But the miracles which I saw and which were recorded, came as I moved amongst the crowd and laid my hands on them one by one. Using Svetlana Souzko, who came originally from Kiev, as my interpreter, I was able to speak with each one individually; then with the assistance of Dr. Joy Harrison, a retired medical doctor from Bath, who tried to check the healings, the results were recorded by Katie. This is how we were able to document so many. Although it does not guarantee accuracy, it does show the wonderful power of God, and that He is still confirming His Word today. That night we saw at least four blind people receive their sight and two who were deaf were delivered, as well as many others, too numerous to mention.

The next night, Saturday, the crowd was much bigger, and to me it seemed as if every unbeliever in the stadium came forward when I made the appeal for salvation. The first to come crowding forward afterwards for healing was an excited little boy. He had a large bulbous opaque growth over the pupils of both eyes. He was so certain that Jesus could heal him, that when I asked him through the interpreter in Russian, "Do you believe?" he shouted out, "Yes", in English! After prayer he could see the video camera at five metres, then the benches at ten metres, then the trees at the back of the stadium, twenty or thirty metres away! His mother told us that before prayer he could only see half a metre, and that with difficulty!

The next was a little worn out, toothless woman, deaf and dumb, who could scarcely move her lower limbs. I prayed, God answered, and she could not only hear and speak, but she leapt up and down to demonstrate! Overwhelmed by happiness, she hugged and kissed us with such evident joy.

After these miracles the people's faith began to increase so that many others were healed. Dr. Joy verified another woman healed of deafness, pain in the lower leg, and cataracts. Amongst those healed were many with deafness, heart trouble, pains in their legs and backs. A little girl dumb from birth really excited us when she began to say in Russian, "Jesus loves me!" We were equally blessed by the woman whose face was completely numb from brain surgery, yet instantly the nerves were healed and the feeling came back. Katie tried to keep a record, but there were still so many, at least eight deaf, two blind, several breast cancers (difficult to verify), many women with their special problems, others with severe leg problems, usually arthritis or rheumatism, who were instantly delivered and could walk and run. I was moved by the man with severe pain in his leg from an old bullet wound. The pain went from his leg and his back!

The next day, Sunday, I was able to speak in the local Church who were supporting us. I love such opportunities because they give me the chance to set the whole church on fire by the power of the Holy Spirit. My call from God is not only to evangelise, but more importantly, to challenge the local believers, to call down the power of the Holy Spirit and to let Him revive the Church so that, after I have gone, they will continue the work and bring revival to the whole region.

At night we were back in the football stadium to find that the news had spread across the town. A bigger crowd than ever streamed through the gates and again they almost all responded to the call for salvation. It clearly seemed that only the believers were left sitting, the rest crowded onto the grass in front of me, hungry in their hearts to know the reality that God can and will forgive all sin. The Word says plainly and I preach, "If you will confess with your mouth the Lord Jesus, and believe in your heart that God raised Him from the dead, you will be saved". Romans 10:9.

As we were walking out of the gates of the stadium on the last day, one of the ministry team from the Church at Ulan Ude stopped me and asked me to pray for him and his wife that the Holy Spirit would anoint them and give them a ministry together. With his eyes shining, talking about all the signs and wonders he had seen in the stadium, he said, "Things like this have never happened in Ulan Ude before!"

This was to set the scene for the nine weeks that would follow. BUT it does not answer the question WHY WERE WE HERE?

Chapter 3

WHY WERE WE HERE?

I had come in response to an unfolding vision. Long before anyone commonly went as missionaries and evangelists into Eastern Europe, I had answered the call of God on my life. It was over thirty-three years ago that I first began to go behind the Iron Curtain as it was then, with my Christian travel company, Crusader Tours, but burning in my heart was the vision of a revival greater than the world has ever seen. After all, the people of Central and Eastern Europe have never, since the day of Christ, seen the real power of God. For nearly two thousand years they have been enslaved by either religion or ideology.

The next step for me was an invitation to speak in one of the 'Underground' Churches in Yugoslavia. Although I crossed the whole of Europe just to preach in one meeting, I ended up by speaking in several different places in that area before returning to England. I met a great many people and got to know their problems first hand. After the services I was asked so many times for Bibles that the few I had brought were gone almost immediately. They begged me to come again, bringing more, since it was impossible to obtain them in their own country. I wanted to help these people who were my brothers and sisters in Christ, even to the extent of involving my travel company and the staff, if they were willing. It seemed obvious to me that, with a fleet of coaches continually visiting these countries, I had a perfect set up for transporting Bibles and other supplies.

Any hesitation I may have had about returning was dispelled by the touching farewell from the young people at that first Church. "We prayed for you to come", they said, "and you came. Now we shall go on praying that you will come again, and you will come."

So the Bible smuggling began, but I could never take enough. I wanted to build a special secret compartment into one of the coaches, take several thousand Bibles each trip, teams to work with me, and most of all, someone to supply the thousands of Bibles, New Testaments, Gospels, hymn books and good Christian literature. It was too big a project for me to handle alone. I asked God to show me the way and open the doors. God answered my prayers! In the next few years I took over 150,000 Bibles and New Testaments before being arrested at the Czech border on midsummer's day 1972, truly the longest day of my life.

Even after my miraculous release from prison in fulfilment of a vision which had revealed the exact day of my release, I continued to burn for Eastern Europe, the last words of one of my fellow prisoners continually ringing in my ears, "No one knows, no one in the West cares." That is why I went around the world for two years telling my story which was so powerful that it was the means of leading over a quarter of a million people to Christ; that is why in 1976 I headed up the successful world-wide campaign to release Georgi Vins, a renowned Russian Pastor from Kiev, sentenced to near certain death for his faith; that is why I continued to go into the Underground Churches to preach and eventually, more and more openly to hold crusades and conferences.

But it was in 1986 that God spoke clearly to me again. Now He told me that the Iron Curtain that had separated East and West Europe for so long would be melted by the Power of the Holy Spirit and that a new great move of the Spirit would sweep across the whole of Europe, uniting East and West, that this would not be an act of man, but a sovereign act of God moving in such demonstration that we would recognise it as only God's Power.

Whenever God tells me something He always expects me to 'put my feet where my mouth is' and act. The vision and prophecy began to be fulfilled when, in 1988, I organised and held a great East-West Conference in Karlsruhe, West Germany. Four thousand came, but the miracle was six hundred delegates who actually managed to cross through the Iron Curtain and attend! This was indeed prophetic of what was to come. I thought I had done my part, but God challenged me to hold another East-West Conference in Karlsruhe the following year, 1989, and to again publicly prophesy the fall of the Curtain. Within weeks of the ending of the conference the Wall began to collapse. God had fulfilled His Word!

But now, in the midst of the world-wide euphoria at this great event God spoke to me again. This time it was a warning. Time is short. Another curtain will fall across Europe first by economic collapse, second by military might and third by spiritual force. The Body of Christ must now rise up in intercession and spiritual warfare to hold back Satan's power long enough for Europe to be saved. Satan is already defeated because Christ has won the Victory. Revival is God's promise. He said, "In the last days I will pour out my Spirit." I stand in faith because, like Paul, "I believe God."

From the collapse of the Wall, the programme of crusades and conferences I had already been holding in Eastern Europe intensified. Everywhere we saw the Power of God fall, just as He had promised, in Hungary, Czechoslovakia, Bulgaria, Poland, Romania, the Ukraine. Amongst the most memorable in the early years was the EuroVision Conference we held in Debrecen, Hungary, in May 1990. For the first time in Church history there we had the support of ALL local Churches - Reformed, Pentecostal,

Baptist, Catholic and Free Churches. We had delegates from Romania, Bulgaria, the Ukraine and other parts of the USSR, from Czechoslovakia, Poland, East Germany, West Germany, America and the United Kingdom, as well as others. Speakers were myself, Dr. Lester Sumrall from America, Ray McCauley from South Africa, John Angelina from West Germany; YWAM sent mime artistes and Vinesong blessed us with their anointed ministry. The Body of Christ was built up, thousands were saved, and many miracles and healings took place in the Name of Jesus!

I shall never forget either the dramatic and exciting crusade we held later that same year in Bulgaria before communism finally collapsed there. Before the crusade even opened, we got permission to hold an open-air service in the big square in front of the Communist Party Head Quarters in Jambol. This city of 100,000 had never seen or witnessed such scenes before. Vinesong joined with other music groups to present a programme which drew the crowds as darkness fell, packing this great square. As Vinesong sang in Bulgarian: "I BOW THE KNEE TO JESUS", the whole crowd, 10,000 strong, knelt in prayer with their hands raised in worship and acceptance of Christ. Even the Communist police on duty took off their hats, and the Communist Party Flag, which until then had been fluttering bravely in the breeze, hung down limp, as if it too were bowing before the Name of Jesus!

What a tremendous start to the Crusade! We saw the sports hall packed not only for the evening meetings with 7000 crowded in, leaving only standing room, but even during the morning and afternoon sessions we found the hall full of people hungry for the Word of God. Bible teaching in the day, followed by evangelistic outreach at night saw over 2000 recorded decisions of people who were counselled and led to know the Lord. For four days we saw and witnessed the mighty power of God, not only in conversions, but also in mighty miracles of healing; night after night crutches were thrown onto the platform as people were delivered and walked out free; the blind, the deaf, the sick - all were healed.

For four years I worked ceaselessly across the whole of Europe preaching the Revival Fire of God, exactly as He had told me to. But He had promised me that at the end of this fourth year, momentous changes would begin to take place. And so they did, in the summer of 1993.

It was going to Chita and Duldurga in Siberia that year that touched my heart. I found here a nation almost totally without God, one of the least evangelised areas of the world; 65 million people, a land mass 52 times that of Great Britain, so large that well over one million square miles of space would be left over if the United States were placed into its centre, 4,000 miles from east to west, 2,000 miles from north to south; a land whose history, under the Czars and under communism, was of exile, prison camps, torture and death, yet where cities of over half a million exist; a land potentially wealthier than America, yet its people die in poverty; a warm, loving, hospitable, caring people, yet for so long tortured, imprisoned and killed.

Now God began to unfold a greater vision and an unprecedented challenge - two years to reach the whole of Siberia for Christ before another curtain comes down to prevent evangelism - a task so large, so tremendous, it can only succeed by a mighty demonstration of the Power of God's Holy Spirit - but because it is God's call and His vision, He will not fail! As God unfolded this new concept to me - His strategy for Siberia - I realised it would require an army of intercessors and street evangelists burning with the zeal of God to work with me, some from the United Kingdom, some from Germany, but the majority would be Russian speaking men and women from the countries of Eastern Europe where I had laboured and harvested for so long.

The response of the East Europeans excited me. In one

Church alone, in Kiev, 100 came forward to give themselves to the vision of evangelising Russia, beginning in Siberia. I told them how hard it would be, living in hostels, only cabbage or potato soup to eat, no proper facilities. They said, "No problem, we live like that here!" Then I said, in Luke 9 and 10 Jesus told His disciples "preach the Gospel, heal the sick, raise the dead!" (see *also Matthew 10:7,8)*; as soon as you get off the airplane, in the streets, schools, hospitals, prisons, cinemas, door to door, you must do the same! They all said "DA!" (Yes!).

I then said we needed them for two months, "DA!", they must leave homes, wives and families, "DA!", bring their own money for food, "DA!", those who stay behind must support the families of those who go, "DA!". We would only pay their air fares. I almost wept to realise how willingly they would obey the Lord, and at what cost. To them Siberia meant punishment, prison, exile, death for their own relatives - but what great love, that these Ukrainians could love the Russians so deeply!

I shared how God had spoken to me from 2 Samuel 5:23-24, that we must begin in the far East of Siberia - the end of the world - that the Revival which will sweep Russia would begin there. I stopped, then three Pastors stood up to confirm what I had said. They told how many prophecies had spoken of Revival beginning in the East. They had not believed - surely Revival will come from America, England, Germany, the West - "Now we understand how these prophecies will be fulfilled, that is why we will go."

Chapter 4

FIRST ENCOUNTER WITH THE ZAVTRA SPIRIT

Now the vision was becoming reality. It is one thing to dream, but it is the reality which counts. God had so impressed on me over the years the importance of never making a statement unless I intended in the power of the Spirit to carry it out. This was one of the reasons behind all my adventures in those early expeditions to Jerusalem which had opened the door for God to use me in Bible smuggling and had taken me so dramatically behind the 'Iron Curtain' as it was in those days, into Bulgaria. I had made a declaration while holding a Crusade in Northern Ireland in 1959 that I would go overland to Jerusalem, to attend a World Conference being held there in 1961. Because I made this confession publicly, God enabled me to fulfil it. Yet the hunger in my heart which had been the reason for going to Jerusalem all those years ago was now still in 1994 the underlying reason for the whole vision which God had burned so deeply into my heart for Siberia: the desire to see the power of God poured out today in greater measure than at Pentecost.

The reason I had wanted to be in Jerusalem in 1961 was that there was to be held that year the first World Pentecostal Conference in Jerusalem, on the day of Pentecost. I was a young Evangelist and Pastor, recently married, with two children and no money! But I had a hunger for the reality of seeing the power of God. If only I could be there on that day. But I had no money for the air fare, so looking at a map of the world, I simply said, ''It's nearly all road between here and Jerusalem, I'll go by car.'' And that is just what I did. But although God was to use this to open the door into so many miracles and confirm my call to Eastern Europe and Russia, the Conference itself was such a disappointment. Unwilling to accept this disillusionment, I began a life-long search for the fulfilment of this dream of seeing all that God had promised in His Word, that would ultimately lead me to believe for the Revival in Siberia.

Now I am in Siberia and the first Crusade in Ulan Ude has been a wonderful opening success, proving that the Lord is really at work miraculously confirming His Word and every promise which He had given me over the past months. It is Monday afternoon and we were booked, so we were told, on the daily 3 o'clock flight to Severobaikalsk. The advance party had set out for the airport with the sound equipment, only to find that Mondays are an exception. The 3.00 pm flight leaves at 11.00 am - so we had missed it! Never mind, we could fly tomorrow and still arrive in time for the evening meeting as it was only a short distance away. Meanwhile we could have the barbecue that Thomas had wanted to give us and he could help us with negotiations for the charter flight we would need to get to Khabarovsk later in the week. Little did we realise in this first slight delay that we had had our first encounter with the Zavtra spirit that would so bedevil us, and with which we were to battle all the way through Siberia. (Zavtra is the Russian word for 'tomorrow' but we used it like the Spanish word 'mañana', literally because tomorrow never comes! Whatever we wanted, from air tickets to visas, the reply so often given was not 'niet' - no - but 'zavtra' - tomorrow.)

So, light-heartedly in the midst of our small crisis, we all set out for the Siberian forest with Thomas in his minibus and two cars.

We had met Thomas the night before at the stadium. I had been preaching, then praying for the sick for over three hours and I really wanted to get away from the crowds and rest. But I noticed one man waiting and waiting, very patiently and away from the others, as if planted in the ground. What was unusual was that, unlike the broken people we were praying for, this man looked strong and well.

When we finally turned to him, his request was that we would go to the hospital and pray for the mother of a friend of his who was dying of cancer. The fact that we went, not once, but three times, showing both love and concern, as well as the fact that there was a dramatic improvement in her condition, secured Thomas's friendship for life.

Now here we were, a team of stranded evangelists having 'shashlik' at a wonderful barbecue with Thomas and his three swarthy Georgian friends. As part of the central team, our light hearted enjoyment of this brief interlude was shared by Rick, Phil, Alex, Dr. Joy, Katie, Svetlana, Olga, and myself. Richard, who was leading Team A as well as helping with the overall organising, was also with us. It was to prove one of the very few opportunities that I would get to relax while in Siberia.

Unlike the long tiring flight from England, our journey out of Ulan Ude on the Tuesday was easy, travelling on a scheduled flight into the indescribable beauty of Severobaikalsk only 500 km (300 miles) away. To me, as the Pastor took me round the following day, it seemed to be very much like Switzerland, only so much bigger. As his car climbed up the hill just a short distance out of the town along the dusty roads, we turned a bend and he stopped for us to get out and admire the view. We were absolutely dazzled by the splendour of the snow capped mountains and Lake Baikal itself, so vast, 400 miles long and between 30 and 45 miles wide, wider than the English Channel which, at its narrowest, is only 21 miles. It is the coldest, deepest inland water in the world, containing one third of all the world's fresh water, edged all round on this side by steep cliffs, forests and snow capped mountains, but on the other by a plateau and the many rivers which feed into the lake. Svetlana, or Svieta as we affectionately call her, decided that if we were ever to open an office in Siberia, Severobaikalsk must be one of the most beautiful locations. Born in Kiev of a Siberian mother and a Belarussian father, Svieta trained for several years in Bible Schools in the Ukraine, Croatia and England before joining our office staff in the U.K.

Returning to the town, the Pastor showed us his new church building which was being constructed by the members in timber from the forests. It would soon be ready for the new converts who would come to accept Christ over those two brief days we would be spending in this earthly paradise. His invitation to return was carefully noted, with my own personal desire to be able to relax here sometime and rest as Jesus did many times during His own ministry.

The blessing of God was on Severobaikalsk, the Pastor, and on our own ground team, Team B, who unlike us were able to spend seventeen days here. The blessing of God was of course also on the Crusade itself. Even in this small town over a thousand came forward to receive Christ in the two nights. God's Word was again confirmed by the mighty miracles of healing. One of the first to come was a bearded man with back and head pain resulting from a spine broken a year ago. As the power of God touched him he showed the joy in his face as he bent right down, all pain gone - a complete miracle which set him free. Then a young mother only twenty-three years old, with two small children was the next in that great crowd pressing forward for prayer. Her left leg had been paralysed from birth, but as I reached out to her, touching her with absolute faith in His power, she was instantly healed and demonstrated by kneeling down, then walking away unaided.

Amongst the crowds whom I was able to deliver by the authority of Jesus' Name was a little nine year old girl with blonde hair. She asked for prayer because of poor sight and pain in her eyes. Not only was she completely healed, she also realised her lifelong stammer had gone and she could speak whole sentences clearly and confidently without stuttering. An old woman who had suffered for twenty-five years from chronic back pain, was instantly delivered, as also was a middle-aged man who had had pain in his hip and side for nine years and in his back for four years, all because of a deformity in his spine. Completely healed of the deformity, all the pain which he had endured so long left him.

In this region are a large number of Buryat people. They are of Mongolian origin, having settled many centuries ago in Siberia as deserters from the Mongolian army of Genghis Khan. (The name Buryat means 'coward'.) In our meeting one of them, a young woman, so beautiful and well dressed, came expectantly to be healed of acute deafness. As I touched her in Jesus' Name, first she could hear 50%, she said, then 75%, then finally 100%!

There were so many other people healed and delivered in those wonderful meetings, but these were the ones we remembered the most on this occasion. Now the beauty of the lovely surroundings of Severobaikalsk was surpassed by the beauty of the One who Himself bore our sicknesses in His own Body. His love and His compassion outshone the glory even of His creation.

Getting into Severobaikalsk from Ulan Ude had been our first encounter with the Zavtra spirit. We were delayed by a day, but still arrived in time. Our second more serious encounter was trying to get from Severobaikalsk to Khabarovsk - we arrived just hours too late for our first meeting. Our third encounter however was to result in a resounding victory....

Chapter 5

ALDAN WAS IMPOSSIBLE TO
GET INTO BUT...

The car bounced over the potholes as we drove up the mountainous road which was the only link between Neryungri and Aldan. The small Russian-built Lada car was only two years old but looked and felt more like ten and was heavily loaded with the driver, my interpreter Svieta, and myself, plus all our baggage and the whole sound system we had borrowed for this Crusade. The road was a typical, unmade, rough gravel track, deeply potholed from the heavy vehicles and extreme weather conditions which varied from plus 30 degrees centigrade to minus 40 degrees. The five hour trip was a nightmare, snow and ice to our side on the mountains, swerving to miss some of the holes, seeing the numbers of sections of burst tyre that marked every hundred yards, ominously reminding us of the fate that had befallen others who had braved this road.

Yet to me this was the fulfilment of one of the greatest miracles of the Siberian Adventure. It was only yesterday morning that I had spent four hours desperately trying to get the tickets in Khabarovsk for the flight which had been booked well in advance for all fifteen of us in the central team to fly up for the Crusade in Aldan via Neryungri.

We had all eagerly anticipated this Crusade because we knew that this was a 'closed' town, which meant that no one was allowed in without a visa. There was no church, apart from a small group of Baptists. Not even the Russian Orthodox had succeeded in establishing a church there. Right from the beginning we had known this and so had thoroughly prepared, getting the Pastor of Neryungri to obtain our group visa well ahead of time, and even block booking the air tickets for the flight. Despite this, the devil had attacked us. The visa had not arrived and appeared still to be with the Pastor in Neryungri, and all attempts to obtain the pre-booked tickets without the visa were in vain. We had tried every possibility in the offices of Aeroflot and the police who controlled the issue of visas, without any success. Both had said an emphatic 'niet'.

I went wearily back to the apartment where the fourteen others in the group sat waiting with their bags all packed expecting the good news. After all God had called me to go, and He never fails, but the look on their faces when I told them was enough. "Right," I said, "we go straight to prayer, God will find a way." Within minutes I stopped them. "God has spoken clearly to me, He has promised that I will get just one visa if I go back now." But this was impossible, because all visas had been refused. Also although we had two ground teams waiting in Aldan, one with about twenty Ukrainians, the other with twelve from Bulgaria - without my interpreter I could not preach! So even one visa would not be enough.

Probably some of the team, like others, would question whether at this point I actually heard God, or whether this was just my imagination. Nevertheless obedient to the voice of the Lord, I asked Svieta to come and drove with the Pastor back to the police office where we had just had our request for visas turned down. Walking in, I saw a young woman officer on duty alone, probably because it was lunch time. When the Pastor handed over my passport with the request for the visa, she complied immediately, stamping it into my passport before even, in her inexperience, asking for the copious forms to be filled in. Taking advantage of the situation we then asked for one for Svieta. The young officer hesitated, then saying that because Svieta was Ukrainian she did not know which type to issue, she went into the inner room to ask her boss. He immediately and angrily refused the visa, making clear that none were to be issued. But we already had mine!

Hurriedly we left the office, understanding exactly what the Lord had said to me, that I would obtain only one visa. But this did not solve the problem of my interpreter. Returning quickly to the apartment where the others waited, I told them the good news of my visa, arranged for the others in the main team to travel in advance to the next Crusade in Blagoveshchensk, and took Svieta with me to the airport. With the visa in my passport it was no problem to purchase my ticket. Amazingly they also let us have a ticket for Svieta without questioning her lack of a visa. Strange, our angels must be working overtime here!

The flight was not direct into Aldan, but to Neryungri. The aircraft was a YAK 40, Russian-built, quite small with surprisingly only thirty-eight seats yet three big jet engines which made it quite fast, so it only took about two and a half hours for a flight of about 1,500 km. We were to see more of these planes later as they are widely used for travel into the smaller airports. So many of the towns we visited had no road or rail connections, and the only practical way in or out was by air. Seeing how dependent they are in Siberia and the Far East on air travel, and also how many aircraft are in use there with such long distances to fly, was to gradually change our whole attitude favourably towards the official airline, Aeroflot, which had earlier been renamed by us as Aeroflop.

Immediately the flight from Khabarovsk touched down at Neryungri airport, the military came on board. Starting at both front and rear, they carefully checked every passenger to see if they had a visa, and that it was in order. More than one did not satisfy these men and the unfortunate person was treated roughly, his passport taken away and the victim removed and placed under arrest until he could be returned back into Khabarovsk. They reached my seat and demanded curtly to see my passport. Svieta reassured them in Russian, as they spoke no English, that my visa was in order, and that we would be going on to Aldan later. The officer, still speaking Russian, asked if Svieta was my interpreter, then by the most amazing miracle, since we were travelling together and I had a visa, they assumed that she had one, and did not even look at her passport. Hallelujah! In that moment God had blinded their eyes. I remembered how that although the Lord had clearly told me only one visa would be issued for Aldan, He knew of course that two of us had to be there!

Leaving the aircraft with our baggage, we and the other passengers found that the airfield was nowhere near the terminal building and it took an unbelievable twenty minute ride over stony mountainous roads before we finally arrived at the remote terminal. Here we were relieved to be met by two men from the local church who took us by car for a further thirty minute ride into the town and to the apartment where we would spend the night. It had been a tiring day, and we were now much further north into the rougher terrain which was characteristic of this part of Northern Siberia.

After a wonderful meal provided by members of a housegroup from the local church, we discovered that our hostess was a refugee who had been evacuated with her husband and son from the area devastated by the 1986 Chernobyl nuclear disaster in the Ukraine. She had found Christ only two months ago. Later in the evening the Pastor joined us and we were able to confirm all the arrangements for the Crusade which would follow in Neryungri one month later, and to finally receive the missing visa which would have allowed the whole of the central team to get into Aldan!

Next morning it seemed that the only way we could complete

the journey into Aldan for the Crusade which would begin that same afternoon, was by car.

Waiting for us in Aldan were the Bulgarian group under our friend of many years, Milcho Totev, whom we know both as Pastor and Evangelist. He was the first Bulgarian to attend the wonderful and prophetic East-West Conference I organised in Karlsruhe, West Germany, in 1988 when the 'Iron Curtain' was still closed. So excited was he, that he returned the following year with forty members of his Church. I have worked with Milcho in evangelism over many years, and together we prepared for and saw the fulfilment of the revival that began in Bulgaria in 1990. Now in 1994 he and his church had eagerly responded to my call, this time to work with us for the revival that is coming now in Russia. He came first to Belarus with us in May, and again he was here with us in Aldan.

Also in Aldan was a Ukrainian team mostly made up of members of one church with their dynamic Pastor, interestingly named Gorbachev. His church had begun only two years ago with just four people, but now it had grown to about one hundred and fifty. Since he and his group were here sacrificially to help us in Siberia, Gorbachev challenged me to include his town of Makeyevka in our series of 17-day crusades in the Ukraine later in the autumn. I said, "If you can come up here with us, I can certainly come to you," - which I did, at the end of September. In the three days I was in the stadium there we saw 4,500 receive Christ and nearly 100 recorded outstanding miracles of healing. His actual church swelled to 500 after only the first two meetings. At a celebration supper after the last meeting Gorbachev said, "We sowed our very best into Siberia, we gave our top people to God this summer, including myself as Pastor, my administrator, my worship leader, leaving my very young church to cope. But God has blessed and now we are reaping the harvest here in our own town!" Then he added, "Next year we will come back to Siberia with you David;

please come back to us!"

Despite the difficulties of this pioneer situation so far north, and problems with communication which meant that the advertising posters had not arrived, this Crusade was a great success. The well trained Bulgarian and Ukrainian teams had worked very hard in street evangelism as well as gaining favour with the local mayor and police. So much so that permission had been given for the opening meeting, scheduled to be held in the Culture House, to be held instead in the open air. Right in front of the hall was a beautiful situation; the police blocked off the streets for the crowds who gathered, and opposite was the local park where the people could sit and listen. The two teams between them had a lot of talent - musicians and singers - so that, despite missing our own praise and worship team, the two meetings were a great blessing. We recorded at least 1,500 who came to listen, and as far as we could tell all who heard came forward to receive Christ. How wonderful, every unbeliever within sound of the Gospel receiving Christ! This for me was the real beginning of the miracles which were to increase with every Crusade from now on.

The healings were too many to detail, especially as my faithful intercessor, Katie, who in every Crusade meeting was to record all the miracles which took place when I prayed with the sick, was one of the main team who had been left behind. But I did note down some of the more outstanding ones like the man who had a broken leg and was instantly healed and the two girls who were brought by their mothers on separate nights. They both had deformed spines and as I laid my hands on them in the Name of Jesus they were completely healed. One of them also received healing for very poor eyesight at the same time.

However the thing which really moved me was the man who came up to us asking, no, pleading for prayer. He had been in one of the many prisons which we were to see and visit here in Siberia, condemned to a long period away from his family. While there he had deliberately and without any hesitation killed two of his fellow prisoners. He even told us the horrible details of how he had done it. He had taken a piece of electric cable and making sharp points on both strands of one end, made two electrodes as he called them. Connecting the wire to the main power supply, he then jabbed the first of his two victims with the electrodes and electrocuted him. Later, having found it so easy, he killed the second victim.

Why he did it no one knows. But as he spoke with us he was in a desperate condition. He was now out of the prison and under great conviction. "I cannot sleep at night," he said. "When I lie down I still see their faces looking at me, even though it happened twenty years ago. I have not slept for years, they keep coming to haunt me. I wish that I had not killed them, they had done nothing wrong, it was all my fault. If only I could tell them that I am sorry and I did not mean to kill them, but I cannot. They are dead and gone. If only I could bring them back and tell them, but it is too late. Please help me if you can." We did help him and showed him the way of forgiveness, so that even a murderer can receive pardon from God if he asks in real sincerity and with true repentance.

This man was one of the reasons why it was so important to establish a new church here in Aldan. We planted a real live, on fire, Holy Spirit church, with a good foundation of new believers who had accepted Christ, as well as some existing Spirit-filled Christians who we discovered were already living in the town. This is where our system of the 'follow-up' was so important. Every Crusade in every town was designed to begin with seven days of preparation by our ground team before I arrived to hold the main stadium or Culture House meetings; then there was to be seven days of follow-up - Bible teaching and instruction of new converts - also led by our ground team in conjunction with the local church. In this case, here in Aldan, there was no church, so we extended the seven days follow-up period in order to establish a church. Our Bulgarian and Ukrainian teams therefore stayed on after I left. They rented a cinema for the meetings and began teaching the new converts on a daily basis as well as continuing the work of evangelism. This new church is strong and growing as a testimony to the power of God.

However, we were back to travelling, and getting out of Aldan was even harder than getting in! We needed another miracle.

Svieta and I had to get down to Blagoveshchensk as quickly as possible to rejoin the central team for the next Crusade. They had had no problem, except that of taking two days and one night to travel by train from Khabarovsk. Our driver from two days before wanted to leave after the evening meeting and drive us overnight down to Neryungri. From Neryungri we hoped to get a flight to Blagoveshchensk. In any case if there were no suitable flight, we had been told that it was only a simple ten hour train journey.

BUT! This is not so easy, remember that we are firstly in Russia and secondly, worse still, in Siberia, 'Zavtra Land'. The first problem was that Svieta and I were too exhausted after the four hour service to face the return journey by car to Neryungri which had taken five hours in daylight and would take much longer in the dark. More serious was Svieta's blunt refusal to go down that very dangerous road at night , and my own realisation that despite the driver's suggestion that we could sleep in the car, the severity of the bumps from the deeply potholed road, which was after all only a rough mountain track, whilst packed like sardines into a tin can with the sound system and our baggage, was a Russian joke.

To Svieta's relief - and mine - we secured seats on a morning flight which we discovered left early next day, Thursday, from

Aldan to Neryungri. No problem, we can then connect by air or, if not, by train to Blagoveshchensk. We flew down and took the ramshackle bus from the landing strip on the by now familiar route for the twenty minute ride to the terminal. Svieta went in and began asking about connecting flights, only to be told that there were no flights from Neryungri to Blagoveshchensk. As for the train, if there were any seats left - and there were none for the next week - the journey took two and a half days, not ten hours!

This was the end! No train and no flights meant no Crusade! All I could do was pray. Once again the Zavtra spirit in Siberia was trying to take control and prevent the power of God from making Jesus Lord of this territory. BUT..! Jesus IS Lord!

I can still see Svieta standing there as I told her to go back to the woman at the information desk who had just told us in the usual rude way that there were no flights. "Ask her again," I said.

"No flights," the woman repeated to Svieta. But within minutes she called her over, "Of course if you want to go by helicopter, there is one leaving in half an hour!" We were eventually led out of the back of the building, through what I can, only describe as an aircraft junk yard. Bits of airplanes lying around, partly repaired planes, ones with either no engines or no wings, take your pick! But if God is in control, and if we really do want a miracle, then we must go by faith.

Then I saw it! A real helicopter, Soviet military style twenty-six seater with the jump wires for the paratroopers still in. More miraculous was that the seats had been stripped out of the interior and two long range fuel tanks fitted, leaving just two hard bench seats. Did we want to fly to Blagoveshchensk in it? Did we! I was so determined to get there that if an angel had come down and tied feathers on to my arms, my only question would have been as to who would carry the luggage!

Eventually an hour later - things never happen on time in 'Zavtra Land' - we and our luggage were loaded, and the four crew members, two women and ourselves waited somewhat anxiously as the jet engines of this fast and powerful machine roared into life. Slowly it taxied away from the junk yard along the ground and towards the real landing strip. Shuddering violently, the machine lifted slowly and, my faith being tested a bit more, we watched the ground fall away from us.

The machine was fast, and the 1000 km flight took only four hours non-stop. Flying at between 1000 and 1500 feet we had a very wonderful view of the terrain. We could see everything, the trees in the forests, hills that made us climb higher to clear them, lakes and rivers, all in minute detail. Even some of the workings of the gold mines are visible from the air, along with other man-made scars which marred the otherwise perfect beauty of the Siberian landscape.

It had been a miracle which took us into Aldan, and it had taken an absolute miracle to get us out. Why was the helicopter flying down to Blagoveshchensk without any apparent motive? Why had it so mysteriously been fitted with long-range fuel tanks? Who had chosen to fly it on the day and the hour that we needed it? And why was it to sit on the ground for days afterwards at Blagoveshchensk with no apparent further purpose? But God does work miracles.

We understood now of course the reason why the other members of the central team had not come to Aldan. They could not have got out! There was only room for the two of us, no more. God had known before He took us up there exactly what kind of miracle would get us out.

Even arriving at Blagoveshchensk itself was another miracle. Our noisy machine vibrated to a stop on arrival, but because of the manner of our departure there had been no opportunity to phone the Pastor to arrange for him to meet us, and because we were not a scheduled flight, no one could possibly know of our arrival. So who told the Pastor to get in his car, drive to the airport and arrive at the exact moment that we did? As I was walking from the helicopter to the terminal he came up to me and simply said, "Hallelujah!"

Chapter 6

A LOOSE CONNECTION WITH CHINA

The relief of actually being in the Crusade city the day before the meetings were to begin was wonderful, as was the fact that the whole of the central team were to be living together in a 'hotel'. This did not mean anything compared to a western hotel. We shared four to a room. The room was very bare with broken lino covering the floor, a dirty mat at each bedside. We hoped that the previous occupants had somehow managed to kill most of the cockroaches which infest these hotels. Fortunately the mosquitoes seemed to sleep during the day, although that gave them more energy for their nocturnal foraging for blood. Did they really have such a preference for our warm English variety, or were they always so vicious?

The welcome sight of an en-suite bathroom was soon tempered by the cracked tiles on the floor, and the crude and almost non-existent seat on the broken china of the object on the far side, whose use was indicated more by smell than by sight. The wash basin loosely identified itself with the wall it precariously leaned against, while the shower tray with its chipped tiles at first gave a hope that at last we would have the ultimate luxury of a shower. This hope was quickly dispelled when one attempted to try the two taps above the open tray. Only the cold tap yielded any moisture, the excuse given, if one dared to ask why there never seemed to be hot water either in the apartments or hotels, was that all heating and hot water comes from a central system which is supposedly 'under repair' all summer. From what some told us, this also appeared to be the excuse given even when, with temperatures 20 to 50 degrees centigrade below zero, there was still no hot water.

On this occasion I shared the room with Rick and Phil. This meant that our room was the one to which the rest of the members of the team gravitated almost continually. You see God had blessed Rick, along with his many other talents, because he had acquired a heating element which plugged into one of the wall sockets - at least the one which was least hazardous, as very few of these were in any way safe. Most of the sockets were highly dangerous with loose wires, broken plastic casings, and some of the working ones were not even fixed to the wall. Rick also had a gift of searching out the local shops where he would buy genuine Russian tea. All that was needed then was to scrounge every available glass from our different rooms. With the element to heat the water, Rick would, with patience, brew excellent cups of tea for us all. We really learned to like very much this liquid gold. I especially, prefer it to the strong bitter English type. The weak but sweet nectar, taken without milk was our main refreshment, cheap and cheerful, and it became a pleasant 'ritual' to meet together last thing at night after a tiring day, or first thing in the morning. Remember that these so called 'hotels', had no restaurant, so there was no other way to get even a drink, except by buying bottles of Cola or lemonade which usually cost anything from $3 to $5 each at the airports we frequented so regularly.

The stadium in Blagoveshchensk was one of the largest and best which we were to experience during our Siberian Adventure. It was not filled however, despite all the hard work by both the ground teams and the local church. Here, as elsewhere, our efforts were somewhat marred by the fact that the local church which had invited us did not receive the co-operation which they should have done from the other local churches.

Nonetheless the first service was greatly blessed and we were to see a real move of God starting here. Our praise and worship team had ministered in the power of the Holy Spirit as usual, under the leadership of Asya who played the keyboard, Gallya and Elena. The girls were supported by Roma, a recently converted drug pusher and addict, who played the guitar and sang. They all had an outstanding testimony of what God had done in their lives, which they individually shared between their songs. After this I ministered with strong conviction so that as the hundreds streamed forward at my appeal to receive Christ, we were once again convinced that every unbeliever in the stadium had come to be saved.

After this it is my custom to pray with the new believers, teaching them their relationship with the Lord, that He loves them and they should love Him and exhorting them both to pray and make an individual and public confession of Christ. I invite the local Pastor to speak with them, then I pray for the sick. First I pray with them collectively, rebuking all demons, false spirits and religions including the ever prevalent witchcraft, and then I proclaim the Lordship of Christ. After that I begin the awesome task of praying with every individual person who is needing ministry and healing, numbering hundreds every night, sometimes thousands. So I invite the local Pastor with members of his church as well as the members of our own supporting teams to help me.

Now we were to see the beginning of new miracles. It seemed that, for this very reason, the Lord had tested my faith so strongly by the difficulties experienced getting in and out of Aldan, and into Blagoveshchensk. Because of the miracles that had occurred with the flights, I now began to see a strong increase in the miracles of healing. We would identify this very positively because of the way in which Katie so meticulously records each person who is healed as I pray. I review these after the service in order to select the most outstanding to share with the people the next night in order to build their faith for more miracles and to glorify God. In Blagoveshchensk we had moved nearer to God and to the fulfilment of all that He had promised for Siberia.

The first to come forward to me was a middle-aged woman, dressed in a red tartan skirt. I remember her so clearly. She was so painfully crippled with arthritis that her husband had to carry her. As I took authority in the Name of Jesus she was released from the pain and began to walk unaided. So dramatic was this healing that we were to see her walk forward on her own the next night, without any help, testifying to the glory of God, and that even as she had heard me speak she had been strengthened again. The next to come that first night was a young woman with blonde hair. She had had an injury to her left eye which had left her blind and with considerable bruising. At the Name of Jesus the 'blind spot' disappeared, then the 'mistiness' went, she told us. Hallelujah, she was healed.

Oh, how can I forget the next, a young boy of nine or ten years! His right foot had been crippled from birth, so I prayed with him. But he would not believe and although I asked, would not try to walk. Of course he knew better than I that he had been born like this, yet I knew in my spirit that he was healed. I literally had to force him to put his crippled foot down on the ground. Without any faith he finally and reluctantly did so. To his amazement he could walk, then with such joy he began to run over the grass in the centre of the stadium, and now nothing could stop him. Even his right arm which had also been weak was healed, so that when he came the next night to glorify God, he was demonstrating his healing by hopping on his right leg then punching me hard with his right arm. So wonderful is God's love and His power!

How can I tell all the miracles of that night! Just let me mention a few, like the deaf woman, the man in his 30's with a spinal problem, the young woman with a headache and severe eye pressure - all instantly healed; also the deaf and dumb boy called Roma - he could hear and speak - and the old woman whose blind right eye was instantly opened. These were only a few of the miracles which we saw.

Saturday dawned clear and warm, the sun bringing the temperature quite high. The crowds in the stadium increased as a result of last night's miracles. Again the anointing of the Spirit came down on us all. This time the young people from the local church under Pastor Sasha led the singing. Oh, what an inspiration these fine young girls were, the pride and joy of Sasha who had specially trained them. The power of the Spirit was so strong on their singing! They danced with the joy of the Lord in their hearts as they sang. Then it happened! Their last song was, 'Poy Hallelujah Gospadu', which means in English 'Sing Hallelujah to the Lord', a song about Revival coming to Russia. I was so moved as the Spirit of God swept over the people, that I wept before the Lord. Standing up as I was introduced to the crowd, I asked the girls to stay, and I asked them to repeat the song, inviting everyone in the stadium, mainly unbelievers, to join in. The whole stadium sang, believer and unbeliever alike and the Holy Spirit fell over the assembled crowds. I was again so moved that when I began to speak, I was overcome for a moment, then said, "When I get to Heaven, I shall search all over and listen for the sound of that song. Then I shall know that I have found all of you here who have found Christ today in the stadium in Blagoveshchensk."

That night was to see again more outstanding miracles. Many healed the night before came back to testify and to praise God. Then the power came down literally right into the midst. A heavily built middle-aged woman whose right leg was broken in two places, limped in with crutches. She was instantly healed and threw them away. A middle-aged man, blind in his left eye from birth, was healed dramatically, then could read a Bible which we gave him. A woman was healed of deafness, and a young man in his 20's or 30's, spastic, his left arm useless from birth, received healing in his arm and crippled fingers. The love and faith in his mother's eyes showed her joy. A ten year old boy received sight in his right eye and lost his stammer; an old woman who had had a stroke and was paralysed on the right side of her face, was completely healed. Then a young boy with damage to his right leg, ran off down the track in the stadium, healed. Next was an old woman healed of blindness and leg pain, then a man, blind in his left eye, received total healing. A young lad who had had an exploratory operation for cancer was healed. He could feel strength surge back into his weakened body. There was a woman too whom Svetlana had met on the bus on the way to the stadium and invited to come. She was healed and gave her life to Christ.

But the miracle which was to be the outstanding one which not only blessed the whole city, but also the mayor, left an indelible impression on all our lives and was an incredible event. A middle-aged man had come forward that night, and I asked him through Svieta what his need was. He had only moments ago received Christ but now he wanted to be set free from smoking. However as I looked at him I saw that he was crippled. His left leg was broken below the knee and his right foot paralysed. As I laid my hands on him and prayed, he straightened up, pulled the cigarettes out of his pocket, stamped on them, and then, to the amazement of everyone in the stadium including myself, ran off down the very large football field, leapt over a high barrier and ran all the way back. This man had a broken left leg and paralysed right foot remember!!

That was on the Saturday night. On the Monday the miracle became even bigger. Pastor Sasha had gone to see the unbelieving mayor, who called out to him across the room, "Hallelujah!" He had been in the stadium and heard me say that I would search throughout Heaven till I found them singing Hallelujah! So he had believed also! Then he said, "What did you do to that man in the stadium on Saturday night? I saw him again on Sunday and he was changed! He's one of the unemployed, homeless problems in my city, unwashed and dressed in rags. But after the miracle I saw him in the stadium yesterday, clean, dressed in a suit and even his hair cut. What did you do to him?''

What a miracle... to us, that the crippled man could run; to the mayor, that a homeless man could have his life transformed!

The miracle of Blagoveshchensk was in fact a great one, because Pastor Sasha had told me that this mayor had refused permission for the Crusade at the beginning. Then only after much prayer on Sasha's part had he said reluctantly, ''Well, only one night. Friday is enough if you want to evangelise.'' Again after much fasting and prayer Sasha had boldly returned to the mayor who then finally agreed to let him have the Crusade in the stadium but only on Friday and Saturday. The official application form was stamped for these two days, but not for Sunday. This had never been changed, although I had agreed with Sasha that we would go ahead and risk the wrath of the authorities. But what the mayor had admitted was that, he who had refused the Sunday meeting, had himself been there on the Saturday, found Christ, seen the miracle, and, despite his having refused permission for the Sunday meeting, had himself attended! For that was where he had seen this homeless cripple in his clean clothes! Now however he was asking Sasha why we weren't continuing the Crusade on the Monday!

But to return to Sunday, a small group of us spent a refreshing time with Pastor Sasha at a nearby lake before the afternoon service. He told us how he was born into a strict Baptist home and how he had always wanted to see the reality of the Bible, the demonstration of the Gospel, the same power and miracles that Jesus did. But he saw nothing. As a result he had rebelled and become involved in crimes so serious that at this very time he should, but for the grace of God, still have been in prison. His original sentence does not end until the year 2004! After serving twelve years, he escaped in 1989, and ended up in Riga, Latvia, where he gave his heart to the Lord. He then of course surrendered himself but began to preach the Gospel there in the prison. Mercifully and unexpectedly he was released in 1991 and went to study in the Bible School in Riga. He had finally moved to Blagoveshchensk just a year ago in 1993 and started the church which was now only nine months old! What an amazing testimony of God's love and power! Despite his terrible past, Sasha was now seeing for himself the reality of the Gospel of Jesus Christ he had so desired to see as a boy.

He also told us that the name of the town, Blagoveshchensk, means in Russian, 'to tell Good News', but that there was a town somewhere in Siberia called, 'Valley of Death'. We were to learn more of this later when we ourselves went to the 'Valley of Death' to hold one of our Crusades.

The Sunday afternoon in the stadium was even better than the previous two days. More people came, the local girls sang with even greater blessing, the power of God came down in greater anointing, and the miracles happened.

The woman who had come on Saturday with multiple fractures to her left leg, returned free of all pain and without her crutches to give glory to God, bringing her husband to be set free from alcoholism! Another woman we had prayed for yesterday also returned to testify of her complete deliverance from kidney stones. Yet another woman, brought out of hospital suffering from violent headache, bad hearing and kidney stone pain, was gloriously set free from the lot! As was a woman also with kidney pain and so severely crippled from the hip that she could only walk with the aid of a stick. She threw her stick away! Several others were then healed of various ailments especially kidney pains; one young man who suffered from heart and kidney disease as well as bad eyes, was instantly delivered of all pain and he could even see properly for the first time.

A little boy came to us with a deformed spine and short left leg. His back was healed so that he could bend and touch his toes and his leg grew out two centimetres! His mother was so moved that she wept and cried as she praised God for the miracle. Another woman healed of a problem with her voice, asked me to come back to Blagoveshchensk to heal all her relatives! I prayed for a man with a lump on the left side of his neck. He had had three operations and been fitted with a special breathing tube in his throat and lost his voice, but under the power of God the lump began to dissolve before our eyes. A mother came with her young son. They both had legs horrendously twisted from calcium deficiency. God totally set them free from the pain. Another little boy, troubled with liver pain, bad eyes and crippled in his left leg due to a missing artery, ran without pain and also instantly received his sight. A middle-aged man who had broken his spine one and a half years ago and could only walk with sticks, walked without pain, unaided.

In the midst of all these miracles came a deformed man in a wheel chair, crippled from birth. For three years he had had such pain in his back he could no longer get up to walk at all, not even with his crutches. I asked him, but he was adamant, he did not want to walk without the crutches, only that the pain would go from his back so that he could get out of the wheel chair! He got exactly what he asked and no more; the back pain went and he got up on his crutches, absolutely thrilled and satisfied. But we were just amazed at his choice to be only partly healed.

Every night in this stadium the crowds had come, hundreds had streamed forward to receive Christ - we believe all the unbelievers accepted Christ - and we saw outstanding miracles in confirmation of the Gospel.

Chapter 7

GOD'S VOICE WAS SO CLEAR

So the Crusade in Blagoveshchensk had come to an end for the central team and we were due to move on. I was determined that this time nothing would go wrong with our travel arrangements. I knew the Pastor and people in our next Crusade town very well. This was one of the places which I had visited a year before. In fact it was in Duldurga that the first idea of the plan for the Siberian Operation had begun. I had sat at the meal table talking with Pastor Sergei about coming back in 1994. Saying that I would bring a full team, we had actually discussed the size of the group, and I well remember that Pastor Sergei had said, "How many will you bring? If the group is going to be large, then they must all have a definite job to do. We don't want them here just as tourists if we are going to sleep and feed them!" This had remained in my mind throughout the planning stages and had helped to formulate the final plan for the team operation. So although Duldurga was not much more than a village, I did not want anything to go wrong since God had really blessed them; they had completed a beautiful church building the previous year, and had established their main Bible School there to train Pastors who would provide critical support for the new churches which we would plant.

We had received much kindness in Duldurga not only from the believers, but also from the manager of the electric generating plant who almost ruled the town. He was so unlike the usual 'communist' boss and had become a genial benefactor, making beautiful play areas for the children and providing special shops where his workers can obtain better food and other supplies at a subsidised cost. His influence pervades the whole atmosphere, probably in turn due very much to the influence of our German friend, Heinrich Buller, Pastor of Missionswerk Jesus Christus in Augsburg, Germany. He was born in the Black Sea area of the Ukraine, and had been deported to the Asbest region of Siberia during the Stalin era because he was of German ethnic origin. Because his wife and family were also all Russian born, their mission works strongly in Russia, as well as other places. It was Heinrich who had made the first contacts for me that had led to Siberia, to Pastor Sergei and to Misha, and who had supported me so strongly over the planning period for these Siberian Crusades.

I thought back to the chain of events which had brought me this far. About three years before, in 1991, Heinrich had invited me to speak at an evangelistic rally in Augsburg. He had then asked me to speak to his Bible School on the Monday morning, saying that there would be some Russian Pastors there, amongst them as it transpired, would be Misha. This young Pastor and administrator who with Andrei co-pastored the church in Chita (not far in Siberian distances from Sergei in Duldurga) was to become not only a close friend, but the main organiser for the whole of the Siberian side of this great Siberian Revival.

The next year while planning the 1992 EuroVision Conference in Karlsruhe, Germany, I had received a request, could we pay for twenty of these Siberian Pastors to come to the Conference? Not realising the significance of God's planning and purpose, but being very responsive in my relationship with the Lord, I had willingly agreed that we would provide food and accommodation. In addition, because of the vast distance to bring them down from Siberia I had made the agreement to pay their air fares as well. Now the Lord was to multiply the seed I had sown and produce in Misha and Sergei the machinery to reap the Harvest Fields of Siberia. How rightly the scripture says, ''Cast thy bread upon the waters, and it shall return unto thee after many days.'' Ecclesiastes 11:1.

To make sure that we would arrive in Duldurga on time I had organised three contingency plans. I had determined the Zavtra spirit was not going to prevail.

The first plan was to try to obtain tickets on a scheduled flight with Aeroflot between the two towns. This however was not as simple as it sounds since, Duldurga having no airport of its own, Chita was the nearest. Chita, unfortunately, had already been a problem to us in our travel to date. All its runways had been unexpectedly dug up for re-surfacing during the whole period of our Crusades in Siberia and had been unable to receive our in-coming international flights. Still, we knew some smaller aircraft were landing on the dirt tracks. From there we would make the five hour journey by road to Duldurga, after a good night's sleep in homes of friends from the Chita Church.

Should that fail, our second plan was already in motion. I had asked our friendly airport at Ulan Ude, who had flown us from there to Khabarovsk earlier, to come and collect us and fly us into Chita. We knew Thomas would help in the negotiations again.

The third plan was the most likely to succeed. Our Pastor friend in Blagoveshchensk had discovered that sitting on the airport runway and available for charter, was a YAK 40, a small, triple jet engined airplane, but specially converted with a good loading door for our equipment in the rear. When Sasha had told me about it I had responded eagerly - this seemed a God-given arrangement!

The devil likes to disrupt everything. We knew in advance that the idea of our breaking his power over an area like Siberia over which he had ruled unchallenged since the time of Genghis

Khan over 700 years before was bound to incur his wrath, especially as the object of our whole Crusade schedule was to uplift and glorify the Name of Jesus and make Him Lord over all Siberia! In doing this we would be destroying the works of the devil. "For this purpose was the Son of God made manifest, that He might destroy the works of the evil one!" 1 John 3:8.

How would the enemy operate this time? I had a clear strategy, three positive lines of approach, strongly supported at all times by the four intercessors who had been part of the central team for this very reason. But we had to wait twenty-four hours, while the whole thing worked out.

By the end of the first day, Monday, Sasha came back to the hotel where we were still waiting. He reported that the first plan, a scheduled flight, was out of the question; there were no scheduled flights into Chita from Blagoveshchensk. Plan two was still possible, but there were problems getting the aircraft into the air, exactly as when we had flown with them the first time; the big airport at Ulan Ude was still refusing permission to overfly and, if it took off, bang, bang, the MIGs would have some target practice! Plan three was evidently the one, but even so we would not get confirmation on that until tomorrow. Ten in the morning, bags all to be ready, wait for the OK.

Tuesday dawned, still very warm and sunny. It was not so much the heat, 30 to 35 degrees centigrade is warm, but the humidity that caused most problems in this southern part of what they call the Far East. I had gone out early this morning as I had found a lovely place to be alone with the Lord in prayer. Sharing a room meant that there was not the opportunity which I craved for quiet times with Him. However, our hotel was only one street and literally three minutes from the river Amur which separated this part of Russia from the vast expanse of China. It seemed quite a strange experience to be so close to the actual border and to find that it was only a simple stretch of water. No massive fortifications, no sign of a military presence, the only indication of a watchful eye was the Russian torpedo boat moored in mid-stream. You can ignore the old second world war gun boat stuck ineffectively on its pedestal overlooking the Chinese side of the river. Why do the Russians stick their surplus war machinery on pedestals in every town and village? The number of tanks and MIG jets dotted in nearly every town and village we entered were almost a form of idolatry. Add to that, the still remaining statues of Lenin, and the statues of soldiers, and even ordinary men and women holding guns, are constant reminders throughout the nation of the controlling spirit, warlike and aggressive that is the symbol of the demon which has until now held power over the lives of these enslaved people whom Christ has called us to bring out of bondage. God's challenge to me for more than twenty years has been, "Let My people go." Exodus 8:1. God has called me to rescue His people, all who will inherit the Kingdom. They are held captive by Satan, and only the Gospel of Christ can release them. As I stood on that river bank so close to China as I had done late last night and now early this morning, alone, yet with God, I looked for a moment, then listened, first to the sound of music, voices and activity that burst out of China and seemed by itself to invade Russia, then to the voice of God. "No, David, not China. Prophecy will be fulfilled not there but in Russia. I have called you for a purpose, which can and will be fulfilled only in Russia."

Now we sat waiting until at a few minutes past ten Sasha appeared at the hotel where we were all expecting the good news. We had prayed and were still confident, confident in God and confident in Sasha, no last minute panic, everything under control, still two possibilities to get to the next Crusade which was to begin at 6.00 pm tonight in Duldurga.

It was the awesome simplicity of the way that Svieta translated the news that made it such stark reality to me. After all I carried the responsibility not only of preaching but of planning the finance, paying all the bills and so much of the organising. No one was able to take this load from me. There was only the responsiveness of some who would spend long hours even amidst the tiredness, lack of sleep and hunger that dogged us all throughout Siberia, to pray not for the team, nor for the transport or the crusades alone, but for me, that God would give me power and authority and keep me so close to Him that I would hear His voice and not the voice of men.

But it was the voice of Svieta which brought the reality. No flights, no planes, nothing. Ulan Ude were still threatening to shoot down the AN 24 propeller aircraft which could have come to collect us, and which could have landed at Chita on the unmade landing strip. And Chita had finally refused permission for the YAK 40 which was ready and waiting for us right here in Blagoveshchensk because, though light, it was a jet.

Absolute impossibility. In simple Russian, 'niet'. Not even as so often we would hear, 'Zavtra', tomorrow, but the awesome simplicity and finality of, 'niet', no. No way into Duldurga.

Thoughts crashed into my brain, tumbling over themselves in their haste to confirm that the devil had won - not this time the Zavtra spirit, but the controlling demon himself. But had he? Without hesitation, as the team were all around me, I called them immediately and urgently to prayer. Not for me the niceties of protocol, God had called me to go. If the devil wants to stop me, then this means war! All out, spiritual warfare, and now!

Within ten minutes I heard the Voice that spoke to me. No confusion, just a command. "Go with Sasha back up to the airport and YOU ask for a plane." I did not question the fact that Sasha had just come from there and that the answer was no. God had clearly said go. One can question whether or not we can hear from God. If this was my human reaction then I would not prevail in this impossible situation. We needed a miracle more than ever before, and only God can work miracles. Had I heard God speak to me?

It took us twenty minutes in the car which Sasha had borrowed, to reach the airport buildings. Svieta whom I had obviously taken as my interpreter waited outside with me and the driver. Sasha took it on himself to go alone back into the office. But I took it on myself to pray powerfully. I found a new sense of power with God and against Satan. I reminded the devil that under Christ I had the authority over all flights and over the controllers of the air space, not him, even if he was the Prince of the power of the air. Ephesians 2:2. I was acting directly under the authority of Christ, therefore had the authority of a greater power than his!

In minutes Sasha was out again, "No, they are still saying no aircraft can fly into Chita." This time I took control and asked to go in with Svieta. Returning to the office he had visited twice before that morning took some little courage, but Sasha had a very strong spirit. Again the request, this time directly from me, "I want to charter an aircraft to fly to Chita."

A somewhat stern official replied rather angrily, saying that he had already told Sasha twice that morning that no aircraft could fly into Chita, that it was Chita that was the problem, he would help if he could, but the refusal from Chita was final. The Voice of the Spirit again spoke to me so quietly, "Ask them for a helicopter. This will take you direct into Duldurga and land in the stadium where the Crusade is to be held."

So I told Svieta to ask them for a helicopter. Immediately the man answered, "Why didn't you ask for a helicopter before? We have an emergency one ready to go, fully fuelled, pilots on standby, it has fourteen seats and a payload of three tons. You can be in the air in thirty minutes!"

Hallelujah! This was an absolute miracle. I knew now that I had heard God's Voice, and I was excited.

Thirty minutes should have been enough, but despite a telephone call to the hotel telling everyone to get ready quickly, we had fourteen people in the team with about forty pieces of baggage, not forgetting the sound system and the music instruments. The total weight was about two tons and required two mini buses, plus a truck for the equipment. This appeared to cause the confusion which resulted in me waiting for over two hours, the papers for the contract already signed and the $6000 paid.

The problem was that Sasha had dismissed all the transport. In his early morning faith he had taken all the equipment up to the airport as early as 8.00, but with the finality of the no, had told the vehicles to go. So it was as late as 3.30 in the afternoon before we finally heard the roar of the motors as this helicopter, similar to the one Svieta and I had used earlier, but without the long range tanks, slowly trundled down the field and with its rather disturbing vibrating roar, let the ground slowly fall away from its feet.

Unfortunately whether it was a direct attack of the devil that we should forget the Crusade and put down in Chita, or whether it was merely the fact that without long range tanks, our seven hour journey was of necessity extended by two stops for fuel, it soon became apparent we would not make it to Duldurga, even taking account of the one hour we would gain crossing back over time zones. The first stop took only thirty minutes to re-fuel, but the second on a remote airstrip in the middle of nowhere was different. There was no one ready to meet us, although the pilots had radioed ahead. We waited a full hour before a second helicopter flew in with some men to man the fuel supply pump. Our Ukrainian air hostesses, the girls from the music team of course, had plenty of time to jump over a fence and buy bread and milk from a neighbouring house, our only refreshment on that journey.

It was obvious we were soon about to be overtaken by darkness. The helicopter pilots did not seem to be reassured when we told them that if we could land directly on the stadium in Duldurga, we had arranged for enough lighting from car headlights and other illumination, to make the landing safe. We could have at least arrived in time for me to speak and pray for the sick, even if we had missed the opening praise and worship. So finally to the dismay of the whole group, and my personal regret, we had to give in to the pilots' concern. Since there was no official landing strip out there the only way was for them to take us into Chita for the night. We were met by faithful Misha and church members, taken for 'chai' (tea) and then to various apartments where we had a chance to sleep. The next day was another battle, to persuade our pilots to fulfil their contract to Duldurga for the original price, but we still had to pay about a million roubles extra in airport fees at Chita for landing and overnight parking. It was afternoon before we finally took off for Duldurga.

Chapter 8

DULDURGA - WE ARRIVED BY HELICOPTER

Our arrival in Duldurga was, despite all, an outstanding highlight of our Siberian Adventure, if we looked at it from the human point of view. Our very large and noisy heli-contraption clattered its way at a height of only about 3000 feet up the valley and over the hills for the short flight between Chita and Duldurga. Hovering over the small town, frightening the livestock, the noisy beast soon attracted all the local children and some of the population. The advertising for the Crusade had been good, but this was the best advert of all! Our ground team, who had spent the previous week there for the evangelism and preparation and who had held the meeting for us last night in our absence, also hurried to the football field along with some of the members of the local church.

We slowly descended, savouring every moment, watching the mixture of consternation and excitement on the ground which was gradually coming into sharp focus as we crowded against the windows. As passengers, we were not hindered by the niceties of such safety features as seat belts, we were travelling Russian style.

The heavy machine touched the ground and stopped its motion but its whirling rotor-blades were still windmilling as the sound of that deafening, never to be forgotten, roar of its motors gave way to the silence of the plateau. Stepping out first, followed quickly by the others, the welcome we received was rapturous.

Filmed and feted, we walked out into one of the most powerful of all the Crusades. We had made it to Duldurga after all and the miracle of our arrival was the precursor to the many miracles which set this small town alight with the power and the glory of God.

That night in the football field - one could hardly call this a stadium - the crowds came in their hundreds, filled the wooden stands, and again all the unsaved came forward to receive Christ. This was our whole reason for being there. Then in the great freedom in the Spirit which marked this meeting, came the power to heal. So convincing and so many were the instant healings that faith for the unobservable was equally high, such as cancer, emotional problems, and bed-wetting with children. There was a greater freedom and power to heal the sick here than anywhere we had been so far, including Blagoveshchensk. Katie and Svieta struggled to stay with me as scribe and interpreter as the crowds demanding healing crushed us until even our clothes were being torn.

The first to be prayed for was an old man with crutches whose right leg was 10 cm shorter than the other. He was instantly healed of stomach and back pain but vanished before we could pray for his leg. He received what he had faith to believe for, no more. Next was a blind woman with cancer in her breast. She felt the lump dissolve and go, then was healed of the severe pain in her head and neck associated with it, and then she received her sight! A small baby in its mothers arms with spinal deformity and paralysis in the leg and foot was completely healed and then to our great joy, two very small boys, brothers, deaf and dumb from birth, immediately both heard and spoke, repeating with wide grins the words which Svieta told them. Their other brother with throat cancer was also instantly delivered and able to swallow. A little dumb girl spoke and another with great pain from stomach disease was set free.

An older woman crippled with arthritis in her legs, hands and elbow was set free, walking and moving all her limbs without stiffness or pain. An old man was so excited when healed of deafness that he hugged me. As he went away he found that the pain in his knees and ankles had gone as well so he came back and hugged me again. A little girl and her mother were both healed of bronchitis, followed by another woman healed of the same, then thrilled because her blindness also instantly went and she could see. Another old woman healed of pain in her left leg, told us she was blind. After we prayed, she too could see! There were so many of these older women troubled with multiple infirmities, yet God saw and answered the hopelessness of their need. The next one was an outstanding miracle - an old woman deaf from birth; she could now hear, then she was instantly healed of blindness! She was surprised and delighted!

So many were healed, we recorded more than forty-five outstanding miracles that one night. But we cannot forget the woman who came, not for healing, but because she had been healed of severe back pain two years before in my Crusade in Mayarki (Odessa) in the Ukraine. Now she lived here in this place in Siberia and she had braved the crush of the crowds waiting to be healed just to give glory to God and bring us blessing from her family. Nor shall I forget the mother who asked me to pray for her sick child in hospital. She told us next day that she had gone straight to the hospital only to find that from that very hour the child was healed, discharged and sent home!

The miracles were so outstanding that Pastor Sergei afterwards took a piece of wood and broke it, saying "Breakthrough!" Then he added, "If the people here see a miracle they believe for life!"

I was to move on the following day, Thursday, for the next Crusade. But because of the disappointment of my arriving a day late Sergei asked me to let the team go on, but stay for another night. This would put my travel arrangements for the next city under pressure. What should I do? As if to finally convince me, the next morning the Chief of Police for the whole region who had given his life to Christ in the Crusade, came to my hotel with his family for prayer. He told us the news had spread throughout all the villages of the power of God. Everywhere they were saying, "David is here and miracles are happening in Jesus' Name!" That is why he had come himself. "If only you would stay one more night, the whole region will come to Christ," he said. I did stay and the power continued to flow under the anointing of the Holy Spirit so that miracles as great and as many took place as the night before.

The crush of needy people around us was tremendous. Svieta was pushed down twice. The story of the woman in the Bible with the issue of blood who had been haemorrhaging for twelve years and who forced her way through the crowds to touch the Lord's clothes and be healed, acquired a new reality! Some quarrelling also broke out among those desperate for prayer - but our God is a gracious God, and He healed them too!

An old woman came, her nerves burning all over her body; as I prayed, cool came over her, all the pain and discomfort left her bones, her back, her feet, her hands. So many people pressed forward. The deaf, the blind, those in great pain, all were healed. 'Noises and voices in the head' were stilled and peace came. Two asked for prayer for the relief of physical and emotional stress after family tragedies. One was a young boy whose father had died and, because of this, his eyes were permanently inflamed. He was healed! Our God is a God who loves us and understands. The second was an old woman. She had had crippled legs for four years, but last year when her son suddenly died, it had got worse. Not only that, but she had become blind through grief. Her legs and her eyes were healed when we prayed! I remember a stocky old Buryat (Mongolian featured) man. His right arm and leg had been paralysed and powerless for fifteen years, but life returned to him, and he stayed not far from us, happily clenching and unclenching his fist for a long time.

Then I was called out of the church where we had been holding the meeting in order to pray for a Buryat woman - only middle-aged - but so severely crippled with arthritis, she could not get out of the car her husband had brought her in. She had been in this terrible condition for fourteen years. Finally, as we ministered to her in Jesus' Name, she was able to swing her legs out of the car and then walk with her husband's help. I was very moved by his devotion to his wife. The crowd had followed me down the steps out of the Church, and this wonderful miracle brought a flood of other healings. Eventually we came to the end. Last of all a Buryat woman came up, just to thank God for her healing the day before!

These wonderful events were still being talked about to the glory of God four months later when I met Sergei the Pastor on one of our planning meetings with Heinrich Buller in Germany. Our God is powerful!

Chapter 9

THIS CRUSADE WAS ON TV

The meeting ended late that night in Duldurga, and afterwards there was a welcome meal supplied by Sergei and the wonderful women of the church. So it was midnight before we got to bed but only 3.00 in the morning when we were awoken to be taken by jeep back to Chita for our onward flight to our next crusade later that same day. We arrived at Misha's an hour earlier than expected, at 7.00 and found Pastor Heinrich Buller from Germany there too. Over a welcome cup of 'chai', whilst the rest of the house tried to sleep on, we shared all about the miracles and showed them the written record.

Misha had us at the airport in plenty of time for our 9 o'clock flight to Irkutsk for Usolye, only to find that the Zavtra spirit had struck again and our flight had been indefinitely delayed. We had a double challenge. First, would we even get tickets? There were none available, we were told. Secondly, if we got tickets, would we arrive in time for the evening meeting? But surely it was God who had wanted us to stay that extra day in Duldurga, and surely it was God who would get us to our destination now? And He did!

We finally arrived at the stadium in Usolye at 6.30, half an hour after the start of the Crusade. Our praise group was already singing and everything was running smoothly. This was the importance of the teams which went on in advance. To cover the whole of the area of Siberia which we were evangelising, covering three time zones, from Bratsk on the west side of Lake Baikal to

Magadan and Sovietskaya Gavan on the Pacific coast in the Far East, necessitated a number of ground teams. Once the programme had got under way, at any one time there were five crusade initiatives running simultaneously. Our co-evangelists had been divided into five teams *(Team A to Team E)*, each of which would stay seventeen days in each location, then move on to the next. They would arrive in the town and do seven days of street evangelism and preparation before I arrived with the main central team, then they assisted me in the actual Evangelistic Crusade which would be either three days, Friday, Saturday and Sunday in a football stadium, or two days, Tuesday and Wednesday in a Cultural Hall, and then they would remain another seven days after I had gone and do the follow-up programme of teaching in conjunction with the local church.

The chart on the following page shows how the system worked.

The ground team in Usolye were excellent. We found they were living in rather grim rooms at the stadium itself under the leadership of Tina Davies from England and Sergei from the Ukraine. This was Team B who had worked in Severobaikalsk and had travelled down to this next Crusade at the end of their first seventeen day period. The difficulties of transport connections were highlighted by the fact that the journey either by road or rail was impracticable, not because of distance but the mountainous terrain which would have involved a journey of at least two days by train, going in a circuitous route as far as Bratsk, then back. So they had chosen the very attractive alternative of travelling down the whole length of Lake Baikal on the jetfoil. When we heard this, we were quite envious, the scenery had been beautiful. I was to fly over this spectacular lake many times, but never managed to actually get on it.

So, here we were, half an hour after the beginning of the first

| 1994 JUN TO AUG | ULAN | SEVER | KHABA | ALDAN | BLAGO | DULDU | USOLY | AMURS | YAKUT | SUSUM | CHITA | UST K | SOVIE | NERYU | MAGAD | KRASN | BRATS |

TOP ROW

The Seventeen Crusade Cities in Siberia and the Russian Far East

A1 Ulan Ude
B1 Severobaikalsk
C1 Khabarovsk
D1 Aldan
E1 Blagoveshchensk
A2 Duldurga
B2 Usolye Sibirskoye
C2 Amursk
D2 Yakutsk
E2 Susuman
A3 Chita
B3 Ust Kut
C3 Sovietskaya Gavan
D3 Neryungri
E3 Magadan
A4 Krasnokamensk
B4 Bratsk

LEFT COLUMN

This shows the days of the Crusades with the date against each Sunday:
Friday 17/6/94 to Sunday 28/8/94.

[The Belarus crusades were in May/June 1994 and the Ukraine crusades were in Sept/Oct 1994]

The shading shows the crusade pattern:
Evangelism   7 days:
Central Crusade 2/3 days:
Follow-up   7 days:

service. Just time for Tina to make me a cup of coffee and straight in to preach. I spoke from Matthew 9, the story of the paralytic who was brought to Jesus. Looking at him, Jesus challenged the people, "Which is easier, to say 'Your sins are forgiven', or to say, 'Rise and walk'? But that you may know that the Son of Man has authority on earth to forgive sins," He then said to the paralytic - "Rise, take up your bed and go home." I told the crowd in the stadium, "Jesus will heal your sicknesses today as the demonstration that He has power to forgive your sins. No man has power to forgive sin, only God, and I will prove it to you that Jesus is alive and forgives your sin when the sick are healed tonight."

And so the healings to demonstrate the forgiveness of sins began. A middle-aged woman and a man in his 60's were instantly healed of deafness; a young lad, dumb from birth, began to speak, his deafness also healed; another middle-aged woman, deaf and dumb, could hear and speak - her little son who had been doing sign language for her was so thrilled! A mother came, a believer for some years we later learned, her blue eyes alight with the love of Christ. She had brought her mentally subnormal teenage son, his expression by contrast despairingly dull and vacant. After we prayed, something of the brightness of his mother's face suddenly lit up his own eyes. The next day he came to us again, this time speaking for himself, inter-reacting with us and other people, saying he felt free inside! Glory to God! Then there was the four week old baby, delicately covered in a fine white veil - only to reveal a horrendously cleft palate and hare lip. We prayed over the little mite, and were so glad to hear next evening that the deformity appeared to be closing over and that, for the first time, the baby could firmly suck a dummy. This was amazing.

I shall always remember six year old Sasha, a grubby, nervous little boy, who handed me a letter. In it his grandmother had listed all his problems for him - that his father was alcoholic, that his mother had abandoned him and that he had a very bad stammer. He was instantly set free, and from that moment, throughout the three crusades, followed me like a shadow. Now he was bouncy and cheerful, and cheeky! He brought his 'babushka' (grandmother) for prayer - the one who had written the note. She had crutches because her right leg was broken and she had pain in both legs. When the power of God fell, she began to skip and clap and demonstrated some Russian dancing! Then she kissed me passionately on the arms and was seen running up and down the track long after she had left us!

A mother and father came weeping with the photograph of their eighteen year old son, in hospital with cancer. They brought the young man himself next day. The pain went from his shoulder where the cancer was, and he walked off, swinging his arm up and round, up and round, enjoying the new freedom of movement. Three months later I received a letter from the young man's father. This is what it said:

Greetings dear David,

I think you remember your visit to Usolye in Siberia and the desperate parents and their son who was ill. You prayed for him to our Lord God that the terrible illness would not touch him. And He has heard our prayer.

Dear David, we often remember the days when you were in our town. When I walk past the stadium, I hear the loud voice with which you magnified Jesus. We are thrilled about your energy and self-sacrifice in serving Jesus. We thank you for sharing in our suffering, and that you pointed the way to Jesus.

We wish you, dear David, good health and success in your noble work. We will pray for you to our Lord God. I remember your shout: "Hallelujah!"

This is the word I want to close my letter with: "Hallelujah!"

Alexander and family

The Crusade was a blessing, but the attendances were marked in hundreds rather than thousands. However, this led to one of the outstanding miracles which in one way or another were to attend every Crusade. The local TV came to film the service on the Sunday. They were really excited and invited me to go the next morning, Monday, at 8.30 am for a further TV interview. The reporter who interviewed me was wonderful. She said how sorry she was that the whole town had not turned out for the Crusade to hear the message of Christ and the Gospel. This is a poor town, she told us, and the growing season is short. The people work all day in the garden - but watch TV in the evenings - so the message will reach the entire population!

The day of the interview she began, "We have the film of the service, so for the first part tell us about yourself personally." This was the opening I needed. I spoke about the miracle of my healing from cancer and of my release from prison. Then she said that people find it difficult to believe the miracles of healing, so I shared again from the scripture all the evidence that healing is for today, confirming it by the wonderful story of when I was preaching in Athens two years previously, how when I had finished speaking in this large church in the centre of Athens with at least 1200 crowding the hall, they brought a young man aged about 25 to me for healing. His right arm was completely crippled, the bones broken in such a way that he could not move it. My Greek interpreter told me that this young man had been studying in the seminary to become a Greek Orthodox priest but in the middle of his training he had wonderfully found Christ and the truth of salvation by faith, not works. As a result he had left the seminary and joined this live church which preached the full Gospel. His own father was so angry that he attacked his son and beat him up, breaking his arm so badly that it was permanently crippled and even his fingers twisted back at right angles. When I saw him, I was so moved that an earthly father could do such a terrible thing to him that I cried out to God, "You are his Heavenly Father, show your love and compassion by healing him now in Jesus' Name." Instantly the young man's arm was healed, the bones knit together, but still the fingers were twisted back, so I took them in my hand and in the Name of Jesus literally straightened them. In that moment he lifted his arm high and demonstrated to the whole church the miracle that had taken place. To my amazement my interpreter, who was a medical doctor, cried out, "This young man was a patient in my hospital and I have seen the X-rays of the broken arm, this is a miracle!"

The interviewer then said, "That is wonderful, now speak to all the people of this large city of one hundred thousand who were not in the Crusade in the stadium, tell them the same message you would have given them in the meeting." What an opportunity the Holy Spirit had given me! I spoke for the next fifteen minutes with an anointing from the Spirit stronger than any that I have ever experienced even in the stadium, preaching the Gospel with power and conviction, then telling the audience that they must act in faith and receive Christ right now. I even prayed with them as they watched the screen so that they could accept and believe. Truly this Crusade finally reached the whole city for Christ, and only in Heaven will we be able to tell the numbers who responded.

Chapter 10

AMURSK - OVERNIGHT BY TRAIN

To get out of Usolye and to the next Crusade in Amursk via Khabarovsk now proved to be a problem. My freedom in the TV studio meant that we were about two hours late leaving town that morning. But I had trusted God that this was His will.

Travelling back by car to the airport at Irkutsk proved interesting because we travelled through several towns en-route, including Angarsk, with block type buildings which, all being painted the same shade of ochre, reminded me very much of the prison I was in many years ago in Czechoslovakia. We learned later that these were indeed former prison camps, all the buildings having been built by the prisoners themselves. Arriving at lunch time we were unable to get a flight to Khabarovsk that day. This meant finding a hotel near to the airport. With all fourteen of us in the team and about two tons of baggage and equipment, we could not move far even to find a hotel now that the cars had gone. Fortunately there was a hotel - of sorts - nearby. We stayed overnight then took the Tuesday morning flight to Khabarovsk. Once again we were met by Pastor Yuri, but found there was no connecting flight to Amursk for the Crusade which was to begin that night. The only way was by an overnight train which would arrive at 6.00 am the next morning.

I will not forget that overnight train journey. The Russian

intercity trains we used were somewhat crude. Other trains like the Trans-Siberian Express which travel internationally are usually of an acceptable or even good standard. However the local ones which we were using were much rougher. Firstly you had to climb up from the level of the track without the benefit of a high platform like we have in England. This was extremely difficult with all our equipment. Then the carriage was rather dirty and very crowded, every place was filled. Usually you had to book days or weeks in advance to get a reservation. Everyone always has so much baggage which then blocks the corridor and most of the compartment. Each compartment sleeps four persons who sit two on each side, then at night these bench seats become a bunk. Above your head instead of a luggage rack is another bunk which folds down giving you two upper and two lower bunks. If you travel first class your extra money purchases a door which gives you some privacy. Second class simply means no door, but instead two extra bunks, one above the other, running lengthways along the corridor. Everyone who wants to use the bathroom day or night pushes past you, along with those who simply walk up and down as part of the pleasure of travelling Russian style. The toilets are best avoided, as in my experience they consist of a china or metal pot which is supposed to discharge direct onto the track below, but the condition of the floor seemed to question this.

If you understood the system or like us had the benefit of Russian speaking members in the team, you were able for an additional payment to get clean sheets and pillow cases with which to disguise the stained and filthy mattress and blanket. Obviously the only food and drink was what you brought with you, none was available. As we settled down for the night, I tried to sleep but the lurching of the train, the unevenness of the track, the sudden jolting as it either braked sharply or moved forward again made this difficult. Eventually, exhausted by the long day and the distance which we had already covered by air, I fell into a fitful sleep. We could not rest easily because we had been advised to get off at a small station which we would probably reach by 6.00 am, if on time. Only Svieta would know which one it was. Soon after 5.30 I was shaken into partial wakefulness by one of the many violent jolts which had disturbed me, only to find that Svieta had come from the next compartment to say that we were due in at any moment and all the beds had to be put down and the sheets returned to the attendant. Still only half awake, I scrambled to do as I was told. No possibility to get to the bathroom as every female in the team was in front of me in the queue. Then the train lurched drunkenly to a halt and we were warned by Svieta we only had two minutes to locate all the forty pieces of baggage, including the music instruments, and part of the sound system, and get off. Since it was only a minor stop, the train would not wait for us to disembark in the normal manner.

As the train disappeared from view, we found ourselves, bodies, bags and baggage standing sleepily by the side of the track in pouring rain. Dawn was just breaking. Some of us had found coats to protect against the weather, others had still got theirs packed into the luggage. It was hardly the time to start searching through suitcases because Svieta said that we had to hurry to catch the only bus which would meet the train and take us from this absolute wilderness to the civilisation of the nearby town.

"What bus?" I wearily asked Svieta, who seemed to be the only person not asleep, and she was not really awake! "What bus do we get on?" Wordlessly she pointed to the vehicle which was now vanishing into the distance. "That was the only one, there won't be another one for hours until the next train comes." The thought of spending the next five or more hours standing in the rain with the other thirteen members of the team, no food or drink, and no shelter from the elements by which it seemed the devil was trying to demoralise us, was not my idea of evangelising Siberia!

Rather desperately and somewhat selfishly I began to pray

out loud, "Oh God help me and deliver me from this!" Within minutes a small Lada Niva, a four seater car appeared down the road and stopped in front of me. I hastily pushed two of the older ladies and Svieta into it and was looking to see who else should go, when I suddenly woke up and remembered that I was supposed to be the evangelist and after all it was MY prayer for deliverance that God had answered by sending this angel with his car! Why had he come to the railway at that time in the morning? We did not know him or he us, nor did he give any explanation as he drove us without hesitation directly to the apartment in Amursk where the members of our ground team were waiting. Then he disappeared.

Warm tea and a telephone soon solved most of our problems as we arranged for some of the ground team to collect the rest of our group. Apparently they had sent a bus for us to the next major station down the line where they had expected us to get off. Realising however that the small station was nearer, the team leader had himself gone there in order to help us get off at the next! He got on the train as we got off without even seeing us - and was then waiting for us with the bus in vain at the next station!

The rest of the team eventually arrived and we straggled on foot to the hotel where we were to stay. For once this was a real hotel with good facilities including a restaurant. The only problem was that we had been promised this at the Russian price which would have been about $4 per person per night but the manager argued that this had not been agreed and we British must pay the full $12, although, as a concession, the Ukrainians in the team could pay $8. This treatment was something we were becoming used to, the fact that Westerners always had to pay anything between two and four times what the Russians had to pay for the same facilities; sometimes the music group and our other Ukrainian team members were allowed Russian prices, other times like this a sort of half-way price. The only explanation given was that the salaries of the Russians were so low that they could not afford anything more, the low price simply covered costs. When Westerners like ourselves came we were there to provide the icing on the cake, extra profit for someone! We could not avoid the surcharge because we had to register and produce our passports, which revealed our nationality. The only time we could get away with only paying Russian prices was if the local Pastor had a church member or someone he knew working there who would make an exception. It did happen, but perhaps I had better not say where and when in case that person gets into trouble when this book is translated into Russian!

It was wonderful to have hot showers after our night on the train and to be able to relax and actually have a meal before the service.

The Crusade that night was to be held in a Culture House. These buildings were one of the good parts of the legacy left by the communists. Usually well built, sometimes really luxurious, they are a cross between a theatre and a cinema. Under the communists they had been used literally for so-called 'culture', whatever the local party determined was good for the inhabitants. Also they were generally used by the local communist party for meetings and rallies, so came ready installed with good lighting and public address systems. The latter were not always good, being inevitably Russian-built equipment; the weakest point would usually be the microphones. Sometimes we could adapt our equipment to work in conjunction with theirs, at other times we used ours in preference. However at least we always knew that there would be something ready for us to hire if needed.

Unfortunately despite all the prayer that had gone up in advance, just before the time we were due to go to the service it really poured. No Pastor to take us, no cars from the church members, and a walk which, although it would only take twenty minutes, meant that because we had no umbrellas, and the rain was definitely torrential, I would go into the service looking like a drowned rat. So again I prayed and asked the Lord for help. To my amazement (shame on you, David, you just prayed, don't you believe in miracles!), I stepped outside and there was a bus waiting. Once again I do not know where it came from or why. This was not a main road, the hotel was about two hundred yards down a private driveway. Others from the hotel as well as us got on it and the driver took us direct to the Crusade hall without asking any questions or asking for any money!

Despite the appalling weather, the Culture House was well filled, and, despite the fatigue of travelling two and a half days to get here, I felt a tremendous liberty to preach the Gospel and to heal the sick. All the unsaved came forward to receive Christ. By the end of the service so much power had gone out from me that I just wanted to get back to the hotel to rest. We were nearly half-way through our programme of Crusades and all this non-stop travelling plus meetings was momentarily taking its toll. One last man came up to me, a middle-aged man, his right hand crippled from a factory accident. Behind me was a table. I leaned back against it, exhausted, allowing it to take my weight. I prayed aloud, "Oh God, I am so tired, I have no strength left. I can't heal this man. But You are never tired. Oh God, You heal him!" At that very instant life surged back into that paralysed hand. So amazing was the restoration and so happy was he, that the man took the microphone we had been using and began to testify to everyone for himself. Then he lifted his hand up high to demonstrate by every possible means that God had made him totally whole!

This meeting resulted in an invitation to speak in a special church service in Komsomolsk, two hours away by bus. In Komsomolsk I stayed in a Jewish Christian home and was fed wonderful food, almost too much to eat. Being concerned for their own rather straightened circumstances, I attempted, through Svieta, to restrain the wife. Maria replied from her heart, "When I appear before God at the judgement seat, I shall be held accountable for how I fed His servants!'' She wanted to bless me so much through her gift of hospitality. And she did bless me.

That night in the church I spoke with great conviction. I said,

I have come to demonstrate the power and the Name of Jesus Christ. Faith translates what we believe into action. Spiritual warfare is not just prayer, it's getting up and doing it! NOTHING is impossible with God. The Holy Ghost brings REVOLUTION. There's a second Pentecost bigger, greater and more powerful than the first and God is waiting to pour this out on the whole of Siberia, the whole of Russia now! God is going to take a whole nation - Russia - and demonstrate His Power in that nation, so that the eyes of the whole world will look and see what God can do. God has never done a miracle so great as what He's about to do now, in Siberia. Never in all history has there been such power as God is about to show here, more than anywhere in the whole world, in the whole of history. Young men, young women, get filled with the power of God! Move with God! A new awakening is beginning. No one loves you like Jesus loves you. He wants to forgive your sins, fill you with His Spirit and His Power. He wants to set you on fire with the Power of God and the gifts of the Holy Ghost till you heal the sick and work miracles in His Name. The Fire will come down on you tonight!

Everyone stood to receive the Power of God, and the miracles flowed in confirmation of the Word I had preached.

Chapter 11

KOMSOMOLSK TO KHABAROVSK BY HYDROFOIL

To get from Komsomolsk to Khabarovsk meant a very slow overnight journey by train, whereas for very little extra cost we could travel up the river Amur. This would be a trip of about eight hours on the hydrofoil; in the opinion of the whole of the central team, a very enjoyable alternative to another night on the train!

We had to be ready and get down early to the landing stage, as no one could book tickets in advance. It seemed to be pay-on-the-spot, and very much first-come-first-served, although apparently someone from the church had a friend or relative who worked in the ticket office and might be able to help us. So we all assembled with our baggage, the various music instruments and the parts of the sound system which we had not already left at other strategic points round Siberia!

Trundling the sound system around with us was an on-going nightmare. Originally it had been taken by a borrowed truck all the way from England for the first part of our Crusades in Belarus in May, and had been left by us there in one of the churches in Pinsk. I had spent a lot of time especially in prayer, and in making enquiries as to how to transport the system, which was very large and very heavy, the thousands of miles from Belarus to Chita in Siberia. The obvious way was to send it by air, expensive, but quick and as I thought, reliable. Speaking to British Airways in

England, asking for a quote, I got a very firm reply. They would give me a price and guarantee delivery to Moscow, but from there on it would be in the hands of Aeroflot. The man I was speaking to was very polite and extremely helpful. "The last consignment we sent to Siberia," he said, "has not been seen or heard of since it left Moscow three months ago." Perhaps after all this was not the best way? I had heard these vague rumours about the Mafia and the wholesale thieving going on, but we are British aren't we, who would dare to steal from us?

In the circumstances I felt that although I believed in miracles, I had better use a little spiritual discretion and reserve my faith for a more deserving cause.

This however still left me with the problem, how to get the sound system up to Siberia. Fortunately the Bible says especially for people like me who have rather more problems to solve than the average Christian, that nothing is impossible with God. Of course there is one solution I forgot to mention, don't ever attempt anything for God! This way you don't get any problems or ever get criticised! Even the devil makes sure that you are not disturbed in the luxury of your armchair Christianity! To return to the point, the Bible does say for those who dare to read it, that the Lord says, "Before they call I will answer, while they are yet speaking will I hear." Isaiah 65:24.

So while I was busy trying to solve the problem my way, the Lord had the answer all the time, waiting for me to find out the inevitable, that my way was not possible. So how would the Lord get me out of my misery and transport the one and a half tons of sound system from Belarus to Siberia? Well, Misha had bought a VW minibus in Germany with a carrying capacity of half a ton, and his brother was going to drive it all the way to Chita for him, over about 5,000 miles of very rough roads. So he of course would bring the sound system with him! One and a half tons of sound system in a half ton van is no problem to a Russian believer - he lives and drives by faith. Fortunately his faith, not mine! But then have you driven on these roads? I have in my own car, and it still has the scars to prove it!

Once in Siberia we still had the enormous problem of manhandling these very large loud speakers, on and off airplanes, to and from stadiums. So quite early on we had left them in Chita after the Crusade in Severobaikalsk, borrowing some smaller ones from Misha's church. Even so, because of the weight and cost of moving even these, we only did so when necessary. If we knew that the meetings were in a Culture House which had a suitable system, we sometimes left ours in the left luggage at Khabarovsk Airport. (In the end we passed through Khabarovsk seven times, so it was a convenient dumping ground.) That is where they were at this moment, waiting to be collected when we flew out next time.

It was one and a half hours before our boat arrived, despite the fact that we had been hustled down there as if it was so urgent. Several boats came and went, the crowds which had been so big that many failed to get on the one they wanted, were gradually melting away, and we still stood patiently. All of us that is except Elena, one of the girls in our music group. Always very alive and friendly, she was standing talking excitedly to the others. The rest of us had not noticed that she was actually poised against part of the landing stage which would be pushed out over the river and on to the boat when it arrived. This in any case was quite safe as it should have been fastened with a chain to the rest of the platform. But this time it was not fastened properly.

I heard the shout, saw something somersault backwards and disappear into the fast flowing river. Quickly we realised that it was Elena herself, and she was in the water some distance below us. It all happened so quickly there was nothing we could do to save the poor girl. What a tragedy, just as we were going to enjoy a special treat, and Elena was looking forward to it more enthusiastically than any of us.

Desperately I looked down and to my surprise, saw her swimming round, soaking wet, but laughing and waving to us with all her usual grace. Fortunately the weather was very warm, and soon she had been rescued. She was none the worse for her adventure. Drying herself and changing her clothes she was ready when a few minutes later our boat arrived and Svieta, who always seemed to know the answer whenever I asked her, said that this was the correct one at last. Of course the other boats had all been going in the other direction anyway, if I had bothered to take proper notice, according to Svieta, but then she was Russian, they understand such things, silly me!

The ride up the river Amur was wonderful. It was warm and sunny, we had brought food with us and were able to buy bottles of Cola on the boat. It was so relaxing to spend these hours enjoying the scenery as we watched Siberia pass by the windows.

We spent the Sunday in Khabarovsk and I spoke in the church meeting from Acts Chapter 1 verse 8. We must receive power and then act on that power. Christ's first and last message to the Church after His death and resurrection was to live in the power and the authority of the Holy Spirit - only then can we achieve what God wants to do. God wants to begin a work in Siberia that will prepare for the return of Jesus Christ. NOTHING is impossible. I said:

First, you must pray, then you must act. Elijah in his day challenged the unbelief of a whole nation. And there is a strong similarity between Israel then and Russia today. The power to change a nation is with God, with Jesus Christ. Elijah called down power on Mount Carmel sufficient to cause nuclear fusion. I have a friend who took a blue stone from Mount Carmel to be tested in an English laboratory. The result - only nuclear fusion could have produced such a stone! But the emphasis in James Chapter 5 is not on the fire, but on the prayer, the fervent, effective prayer of a righteous man. God wants to turn the whole of Siberia back to Him, but it is filled with unbelief and false religions. God wants to bring a demonstration of His Power that will turn the whole nation back to Him through you. The people followed Jesus because of the miracles. You must go out and do the same. The Power of the Holy Spirit is the power to work these miracles. Cry out to God and He will give you another Pentecost. The miracles we have seen here in Siberia are only the beginning. That is why I have come, whatever the cost, whatever the sacrifice, to call down the power so that YOU can win your nation. God will give the victory when you go to prayer. He will send an outpouring of the Holy Spirit greater than ever before. I want to give you a vision of what God will do through you. Get on your knees, and then get up off your knees and do it!

Chapter 12

SUSUMAN - THE GOLD MINE

It was trying to buy tickets for Susuman from Khabarovsk that was now proving a problem. Once again we had tried to get someone in advance to make the reservations. It seemed so difficult because of the Russian system and lack of adequate computerisation. Out here in the far side of Siberia it was impossible to book a return ticket to anywhere, or even to make a forward reservation from any airport other than the one in which we were at the time. When I asked for a return ticket to any other city the reply was that they could only quote departures from their own location, their computer could not show what return flights were available. We would have to go to that airport, even if it were 500 or 1,000 miles away to make the booking! It was the same with trying to make forward reservations, they could only give us details of what departures they had, nothing else. I nearly managed to overcome this nightmare once, thinking that I had found the answer, but in practice the system still beat me. I did have a copy of the Aeroflot timetable, but it was no use at all, so in the end I gave it away as a souvenir.

Apparently we had now run into the holiday period and Russians were booking up all the flights! Also, airfares had been steadily increasing in price all the time we were in Siberia. This now meant, that with typical Soviet style logic, because the fares were too high for many people to travel, they reduced the number of flights, thus causing overcrowding and making it impossible for many of us, especially groups like ours, to find seats. In some cases where there had been as many as three flights between some cities per day, they were now down to one; in others from flying daily, they were down to two or three times per week, obviously never on the days we wanted! Add to this confusion, the very high price of petrol, and lack of road or rail communications between most of the cities we visited, meant that even for the poorer Russians air travel was the only possible way to visit relatives or move around.

The answer we received was very definite, there were no tickets available for the first stage of the journey from Khabarovsk where we were to Susuman. We needed to take an overnight flight north into Magadan, then a connecting flight into Susuman, approximately 300 miles inland from there. Flights were going every night, but no seats for us for the next two weeks!

As usual I began to pray, believing strongly that God had promised and He would not fail. So many times similar to this a miracle had occurred at the last minute. It was the Pastor who had promised that a member of his church might somehow find some tickets for the next night, Monday, but I was concerned because that would mean arriving on the Tuesday morning at Magadan with no sleep, and still uncertain as to the connection from there to the Crusade which would begin in Susuman that same night. I could not and would not miss an opening meeting again. It was 11.00 pm Sunday night when the Pastor arrived suddenly at the apartment where some of us were staying and announced he had two tickets for the next flight leaving at 4.00 am! Not much time to organise, but these tickets were the answer to my prayer.

It had already been arranged that our central team would split up a little at this stage. Because Team C, the ground team covering this South-East area of Siberia had been expelled by the police for preaching in the streets, we had no ground team to do the advance preparation in the town of Sovietskaya Gavan, on the Pacific coast. One of our team who normally dealt with the follow-up had volunteered to go there with Olga one of our interpreters. Two excellent German intercessor-evangelists, Reinhard and Suzanna, who had somehow escaped from being tarred with the same brush as the rest of Team C, had already gone in ahead and had already begun preparation. Meanwhile the others in the central team would now go direct by train to the next Crusade city after Susuman which was Chita, and help to organise a big 'March for Jesus', as well as prepare for the meetings. This meant that Svetlana and I could go with these tickets to Susuman, where we knew that we had very strong support from two ground teams, under the leadership of my good friends Boris and Oleg from Kiev, and Kai and Patti from our German office in Weingarten.

So after snatching just a few hours' rest, Svetlana and I set out on the next step of this Siberian Adventure. The local Pastor's car had completely broken down and no taxis were available as we left the apartment at 1.00 am to attempt to get to the airport. The only way was to go to the nearest main road and hope to travel 'Russian' style. This means that you stand in the road and hail the first private car to come by. We did this, not knowing what would happen after 1.00 in the morning. We did not have to wait long before a car appeared, responded to our frantic waving and stopped. Svieta had warned me in advance not to speak in English, so she demanded that the driver take us to the airport, some thirty minute drive away, which he did without hesitation. After we had unloaded our bags some roubles appeared to change hands under Svetlana's direction, then a satisfied car owner drove away and that was it, so easy! The reason why I had to take the appearance of a deaf mute, was that if the driver had known a Westerner was in the car the price would have not only quadrupled, but he would have demanded some large sum in dollars!

Now back once more at this airport which we were to visit seven times in all, it was so simple. Go to the Intourist section, check in and wait until 4.00 am. 'Niet problem!'

After a reasonable flight, no food or drink served of course, we had our first glimpse of the notorious Magadan from the air before we touched down on the runway at 7.00 am. There was a chill about the whole place, not just because of its ugly history, but because at that time in the morning the temperature was only just three degrees above freezing. We had come from the humid heat of the Southern part of Siberia where temperatures were averaging between 35 and 40 degrees above zero centigrade, so our warmer clothes were still packed in our bags. We shivered in the cold air.

But it was not just the temperature which made us shiver - this was the place where Solzhenitsyn the famous author of the 'Gulag' books had once been imprisoned and where it is estimated that up to ten million of those exterminated under Stalin had died. On this occasion we did not go into the town which was over an hour away by car. Oleg one of the Pastor's assistants from the Magadan Church was waiting to greet us. Before putting us on the flight to Susuman we organised much of the detail for the next few days with him, including the fact that he would bring a praise and worship team over from his Church for the Crusade which would begin the next day.

For this part of the journey we flew in one of the many YAK 40 airplanes we found in use in this more remote part of Siberia. With only thirty-eight seats and very little luggage space, this small three engined jet was quite fast but needed relatively little space to land, so was ideal as commuter transport between these far flung outposts of the vast former Soviet Empire. Our only problem was the seats; they were very uncomfortable because they had low backs and no head rests. Also like most of these internal flights, there were once again no facilities to provide any food or drink.

On arrival at the small airport at Susuman we were so pleased to be met by the welcoming smiles and willing hands of our friends from Weingarten and Kiev. The team from Kiev came from

Anatoli's Church. Anatoli was a Pastor whom the Lord had used to open so many doors for me into the Ukraine. I remember the first crusade which I held in Kiev in January 1991; Anatoli had asked me to speak on a Sunday afternoon. With only 150 members in his newly formed Church, he had nonetheless gathered a large crowd. From there on the Lord had sealed a relationship between us in the Spirit which enabled our ministries to grow together.

Later, invited by a group of Kiev Churches to hold a major crusade in their Dynamo football stadium, I found that, through a breakdown of communications, they had failed to organise it. With only three weeks in which to prepare, Anatoli stepped in, demonstrating the power of prayer and fasting, and organised one of our most successful crusades up to that time in Kiev. The following year, in 1993, we worked together in the most amazing EuroVision Conference in the 10,000 seat Sport Palace in Kiev. This culminated in the miracle of the confrontation with the minister of religious affairs in Kiev and a triumphant public victory in Jesus' Name, enabling us to take the big Dynamo Kiev Stadium. The police who had ringed the stadium on the Saturday afternoon to prevent us going in, were personally instructed at the last minute by the minister himself to back down and allow us to hold the meeting as planned.

Now, in response to my appeal, Anatoli had sent over 200 Ukrainians to help me in Siberia, of whom this team in Susuman was one group under the capable leadership of Boris and Oleg.

Our team from Weingarten was led by Kai and Patti Fassbender. Weingarten is a small but very beautiful village just outside Karlsruhe, where we have our EuroVision German office. Christoph and Martha Scheel not only pastor a wonderful Spirit-filled fellowship in Weingarten, but have supported EuroVision since I held the first East-West Conference in Karlsruhe in 1988. Our office is situated in the large beautiful building called

'Maranatha Haus' where their church is, and several church members with other German friends under the leadership of Kai and Patti were members of the team; so I knew them well.

This was to be one of the most special of all the Crusades - wonderful to come into the relaxed atmosphere and well organised routine of our friends. For the first time since arriving in Siberia, I felt the pressures lifted off me for a while. Susuman was not the most beautiful of the places we visited, but so singularly marked by the power of God that it was different from any other town. If it had not been for the warmth of the sun and the temperature by now in the mid-thirties, in contrast to 300 miles away in Magadan, the place would have been entirely without colour.

The main industry was mining. This meant that the residue from the mines covered everything with dust in the dry heat. The gold mine which dominated everything financially was not very evident but the coal mine left a black trail on the roads and fields, even the buildings were not immune. The town was quite recent and the buildings in many cases only five years old and less but you would never realise this from their decrepit appearance. Everywhere were these identical apartment blocks. Because of the permafrost which even in the heat of summer was only about 30 cm (12 inches) below ground level, all the buildings were built precariously balanced on what looked like stilts, which lifted them between one and three feet off the ground. This however was not what attracted my attention so much as the sight of the six or eight storey blocks towering above. Built in normal Russian fashion exactly the same as in every former communist country, they were made of pre-cast concrete sections representing whole sides or ends of apartments, hoisted into position by an enormous crane, then secured by metal bolts. Because of the combination of humidity and temperatures which varied from 40 degrees above to as much as 50 degrees below zero centigrade, these sections were literally splitting apart with great cracks appearing between them.

In an attempt to make them look better and reduce heat loss, cement and insulation material had been plastered over these cracks, surely only a cosmetic repair. I remember walking between two buildings on the ground, through a space of six or eight feet which formed a communication between them. It was when I looked up I realised that at the top the buildings had moved so much that they were actually touching!

Along with the others on the team I stayed in one of these blocks. They had usable toilets and a communal shower, although inevitably no hot water. A short rest, some food brought all the way from Germany and real coffee, and I was ready to look at the arrangements made for the services in the football stadium, sorry, football field, for this was to be the poorest of all the sites so far. It was big enough for the small town of only 10,000 population, but in keeping with the rest of the amenities, was just a basic dusty ground with a large wooden building at one side containing the offices, a gym with training facilities and a small indoor sports room. It boasted a wooden veranda which would act as the stage for us as well as some form of protection from the crowds who would besiege us later.

Svieta had come with me to look at the facilities, so through her I was able to talk to the secretary in the office and found out some interesting information about the town. Her husband worked in the gold mine which seemed to be the main reason for the town's existence for eight months of the year, the other four months being just too cold. The mine which was controlled with very strict security by officials in Moscow seemed to provide the main source of employment, along with the coal mine. The rest of the town must have been totally dependent on the miners and their families. They obviously needed schools, a hospital, shops and so on. Possibly some limited farming took place in the vast open spaces surrounding the town, but with the very short summer lasting only three to four months, and the ever present permafrost, not much could be done. I think that it was even too difficult to grow potatoes this far north. The landscape itself was very barren, not many trees, more of an open plateau, surrounded by the hills which we had flown over on the way in this morning.

The football club secretary was very pleased to talk to Svieta, because they were both from the Ukraine, as were so many others in that wilderness. She told us that although the mine had sent one and a half tons of gold to Moscow this year, her husband and the other miners had not been paid for twelve months. Normally they got paid at the end of the season and in view of the difficult climate and remoteness of the location their wages were high.   No prisoners working here for slave labour, they had been attracted by the prospect of earning as much as four million roubles per year. At the exchange rate prevalent then, it would have represented about $2000 p.a. or $165 per month. This was good, and some told me that they came from the Ukraine, where an average salary at that time was only $20 per month, to places like this simply to earn money fast for a few years, then return home. She and her husband had done it for this reason, only now they would not be able to even afford the fare back to the Ukraine, which I knew was at least one and a half million roubles and going up all the time. Probably it would increase to two million by the end of the year.

We asked her how they managed to live, because everything was so expensive, with neither food nor clothing being produced locally, except what some of them managed to grow on small plots of land, or tomatoes in window boxes. No one incidentally had a greenhouse as there was no means of heating it. Everything had to be flown in from the south, or even further, at great cost. Even potatoes could cost as much as $9 per kilo. She told us that her wage from the club was 200,000 roubles per month and her husband received a subsistence allowance from the mine of the same, making a total joint income of 400,000 roubles per month. But food for the two of them cost 700,000 per month without allowing for the cost of rent, heating, clothes and all the other living expenses. No wonder they said that they would not be able to afford the air fare to go home. How did they live?

As I left the field I watched the intercessors in the ground team walking round the area, claiming the land and claiming souls, in the Name of Jesus. This spiritual warfare was such an important part of the evangelism. The teams here in Susuman had shown me a great lesson in discipline as they had split into different groups individually covering intercession, street evangelism, leaflet distribution and advertising. I was very encouraged and in my spirit knew that there would be a great move of God here.

The morning of the Crusade dawned bright and clear, as did most days that summer! Getting out of bed to go to the early meeting for praise and worship with the team proved so simple, as I realised - with such a song of joy and thankfulness to the Lord - no hassle over travel - I had actually arrived here the day before the Crusade! With the efficiency of the ground team, who were organising everything, I had nothing to do except relax, seek the Lord, and prepare for the meeting!

To me, there was a very strong sense of the Lord's presence and I knew two things in my heart. One was that I was very conscious of our need for constant intercession day and night, which we had, praise God! I was so thankful for our intercessors, both those back home and the ones whom God had laid on my heart to bring with me as part of the central team. The fact that I was separated from these at the moment reminded me that they would be praying even more powerfully. The other was that the Lord had given me a strong sense of victory over the devil. This was to become a turning point in many ways. From now on we would see even more miracles, especially as, just before leaving Khabarovsk, the devil had attacked me strongly, forcing me into real spiritual warfare until I knew he was defeated.

Of course Svieta and I had not attempted to bring the sound system! Instead the local Culture House were lending us theirs free of charge! This really was a miracle, because even when the system did not work as efficiently as it should on the opening night, they sent to another place many miles away and brought a better system to replace it, also free of charge. In addition the lady who owned the local hotel had said that from today she would provide free meals for the whole team throughout the Crusade - which she did, even giving us a meal at midnight after we had finished praying for the sick! Just think, she provided more than thirty of us with three full cooked meals a day, breakfast, lunch and supper, for three days!

I arrived at the football field well before the meeting. Well, it would be dry and thirsty work out there, probably over 30 degrees centigrade and the field had no grass, just dirt and dust, and since I had developed a liking for hot sweet Russian tea, the secretary had volunteered to make some for me before the meeting!

The service began at 6.00 which was a little early as many did not finish work until 5.00, so it was interesting for me to watch the crowds streaming into the field while the praise and worship team, which Oleg had brought from Magadan, ministered in song. I started to speak as soon as most of the 1000 who gathered that night had arrived. The response was tremendous, every unbeliever coming forward to receive Christ, crowding up to the hastily formed barriers. Then after instructing them in the usual way I began to pray for the numbers of sick and crippled who had gathered in desperate hope of healing. Although I first pray collectively, breaking the power of Satan which brings such suffering, I love to get amongst the people individually and heal their sicknesses by the authority given me in Jesus' Name! Luke 9:1-2. Unfortunately, while Svieta was with me as interpreter, I missed the team member who normally so faithfully recorded every case of healing for me. With so many being healed amongst the crowd I can only remember the most outstanding. A man and woman who were paralysed were healed instantly, as was a woman who had been brought from the hospital with crippled legs, able to walk only with great pain and the aid of a stick. This is where the biggest miracle of all began. This woman was so excited by her own healing, that at the end of the meeting she asked me to go into the hospital next day to pray with the other patients.

Going by taxi to the hospital next morning, she was waiting on the steps outside. Completely healed, she could walk freely and without any pain as she took me up the crude concrete stairs, chipped and broken, covered only with thick layers of paint, along the corridors laid with tiles which were cracked and fractured, and into the first ward. Looking around at the men lying on their beds in this room I realised the need. Although the staff in these hospitals are caring and there seemed to be freedom for relatives and friends to visit and bring food, it was the poor equipment and lack of drugs and medicines which gave an atmosphere of hopelessness. There was obviously a shortage of money, but was this an excuse for the sheets and bedding stained with blood and all the other reminders of the length of a patient's stay which I found in some hospitals?

I prayed for the man on the bed on my right as I entered who had multiple sclerosis. He was the one I had been brought in to meet, but he had no real belief. Next to the window was another man. I talked with him through Svieta, asking why he was there. He told me that his back was broken so I laid my hands on him, immediately all the pain left, he straightened himself and got up and ran off to make a cup of tea for me! By now the news of what God was doing was spreading, and another man who was almost blind came from a different room. As I laid my hands on his eyes, they opened and he could see. Someone brought a Bible which was by the side of one of the beds and he read it excitedly, shouting in his enthusiasm for all to hear, ''I can see, look I can read!''

I do not believe that God called me into the hospital to heal everyone, but through these few cases to demonstrate the authority of God's Word, the power of the Holy Spirit and to glorify the Name of Jesus. Shortly after, the lady who had been healed the previous night told me that a taxi was waiting and as I left, she said that she and her husband wanted to pay for it in gratitude for what God had done.

The previous day we had had to face the inevitable question about the next Crusade. Having got into Susuman, how do we get out? We knew that we could get seats on the flight from Magadan back to Khabarovsk, but the flight would leave from Magadan at about 1.40 am on the Thursday which meant that we had to fly out of Susuman immediately after the Crusade service on the Wednesday night. Until recently there had been three flights a day into Magadan, and it would have been no problem, but now there was only one and that left at about 3.00 in the afternoon. Impossible for me because of the Crusade! Asking the team to join me in prayer I took Svieta and went to see the airport director.

He had no aircraft available so we could not charter. I told him the situation and asked if he could by any means delay the return flight until about 9.00 pm to allow me time to hastily finish the service and go. The answer was not an immediate no, but returning after lunch, the authorities in Magadan had refused because some on the flight had onward connections. I was disappointed, because I had felt that this was a simple way to solve the problem, after all God has power to change things and I am never afraid to ask!

That night's service was even more powerful, about 1500 came. Amongst the many miracles, which of course I could not record, I remember a twelve year old boy, crippled and with crutches. He threw them away and was miraculously healed while I was still speaking. There was also the army lieutenant I had noticed earlier helping to hold back the crowds. As Svieta asked why he needed prayer, he showed me two bullet wounds, one in his leg and the other in his foot. Instantly healed, he ran off the field!

After the meeting I went with Svieta, who was very tired, on one of our many similar exhausting expeditions to try to phone our office in England. It was already 11.00 pm for us out here in Siberia, but back in England 12.00 midday. There were no phones in the hostel where we were staying and the only way to call home, as in almost every city we were in, was to go to the telephone section of the local post office which stayed open, in this case until midnight, queue up to book a call, and then wait an hour for it to come through. This meant that it was after midnight when we finally got back to the hotel for supper, even then to find that we were the first in! Having continued to pray for the sick, some of the team went straight to bed, but the rest followed us in, then after a wonderful meal together we all returned wearily but excitedly to the hostel to sleep for a few hours.

Unable to travel out the previous night to connect with today's flight out of Magadan, we were now booked to fly at 3.00 pm. This at least meant that I could go and talk to the mayor who had invited me to come to his office. He told the four of us who went in that he was not a believer and that the Orthodox Church and the communists had tried to persuade him not to allow us to hold the Crusade. "I did not listen to them," he said, "I told them that if you could help us spiritually in the town and also help to reduce the problem we have with crime, that you should be free to come. By the way, I heard what happened in the hospital yesterday, thank you for emptying one of the wards!"

He told us that while until recently there had been little crime in this small community of 10,000, with the problem of unemployment and unpaid wages, crime was increasing. Significantly he told us, "People are in an unsettled period of transition from the difficulties under communism to an uncertain and maybe worse future. You have given our people faith and hope." That was wonderful, coming from an unbelieving mayor.

Going to the hotel for our lunch we were asked to pray for some of the members of the staff who had various physical problems, and they pleaded with me to come back, saying, "You can stay here in the hotel free if you will come back." All this made me a little late, so hastily collecting our bags, Svieta and I took a taxi to the airport. The driver absolutely refused to take any money, and when I asked if he had been in the meetings he said, "No, I wanted to come but could not because of my work but I have heard of all that God has done through you and I won't take any money from you."

Going into the airport for the inevitable hassle of the check-in, the woman behind the desk said, "I could not get to the meetings but I heard of all the miracles, please pray for me, I have breast cancer." She took us into a small room where I laid my hands on her in Jesus' Name, believing for the miracle which would heal her. In gratitude she took our tickets and completed all the formalities quickly while we waited.

As the Russian built YAK 40 soared into the cloudless sky late that afternoon I pondered and rejoiced in the wonder of a God who is so great and works such outstanding miracles. He had changed the lives not only of the mayor, the taxi driver and the hotel owner, but in two days 25% of the whole town had come forward to make a decision for Christ! I had left behind a new Church where before there was none. My soul had wings that afternoon and it soared to a far greater height than the airplane, powered not by jet engines, but by praise and gratitude to the One whom I love more than anyone else in the whole world.

Chapter 13

SUSUMAN TO CHITA VIA MAGADAN

The aircraft came to a standstill on the runway at Magadan. The relaxation of Susuman was behind me and I was now to face the realities of Siberia again. Unable to get a flight out of Magadan meant that today, Thursday, I had only taken the first part of a very long journey to the next Crusade at Chita. It was already nearly 5.00 pm and the Aeroflot offices, which were the only way to enquire about chartering a plane, would be closing. One major problem with Magadan was that outside of the bigger population areas in the Far East, these remoter towns were very expensive. Everything costs more here. Air tickets are not priced on mileage alone, but either on demand or, more likely as I discovered later, Government policy. Why were tickets two or three times more expensive here than any where else in this region? Even a bottle of carbonated drink such as Cola, or some orange or other fruit drink which would cost the equivalent of $2 elsewhere, cost $5 here in the airport.

Vladimir Zhirinovsky who was to visit here shortly after this gave a very strong reason why, and will probably win the next election in 1996 as President of Russia, based on what he said. As we saw in Susuman and here in Magadan, the government in Moscow chose to ignore the plight of these outposts in Siberia. Western help flowed copiously into Moscow as did the wealth created in these Eastern outposts but nothing flowed back in their direction. Neither Western dollars nor even the wages of the gold miners! To make it more obvious even the airfares were inflated to isolate these newly created 'financial prisons'.

My only possibilities for getting out of Magadan were either to take the overnight flight down to Khabarovsk, which would still leave me a major problem as to how to get from there to Chita, or there was another airline flying into Blagoveshchensk next day at 11.00 am where I would again be stranded. To start, I reserved two seats on the overnight flight back to Khabarovsk, but I knew this could not get us to Chita in time. Then Svieta and I talked to the directors of the other airline flying into Blagoveshchensk to ask if we could fly with them, and then charter their same aircraft for the relatively short onward flight, less than 1,000 miles into Chita. We were told that we would have to be in the airport before 9.00 am the next morning to get an answer to that. In the meantime the lady in the Intourist or 'International' section suddenly drew our attention to a young man who she said, could offer us a charter plane. Aeroflot was closed for the night by now. This man offered us a charter, but at a horrific price, $18,000 just for the two of us. See what I mean about the prices!

It was now 8.00 pm and we could do nothing more. In any case a very kind police officer coming off duty at the airport had been waiting over an hour to take us the sixty minute long drive into Magadan, so that we could find a hotel and get some sleep. He was willing to take us in his car for the same price as the airport bus, which of course had left hours ago, and would be much cheaper than the exorbitant taxi fare.

The ride was as pleasant as could be expected in the thirty year old Moskvich car, ourselves and one other passenger, with the bits of our baggage which would not fit into the boot, piled on top of us. I was aware of course that these cars had been imported into England thirty years ago and then been banned by the Ministry of

Transport as they were too dangerous. But never mind, there were plenty of them still around here in Russia. Obviously they had not all been involved in accidents or fallen apart.

It was my first time in the infamous city of Magadan, but as it was now quite late our only thought was a hotel and a meal; we must catch the bus back to the airport at 7.45 am next morning for what was likely to be a hard day's negotiating and travelling, as it would be Friday already and my Crusade in Chita would start that same night.

At the airport next morning, things were clearly not working out. Last night we had told the man with the charter that $18,000 was ridiculous, but we still must now contact the other airline at 9.00 am to see if we can fly into Blagoveshchensk on the 11.00 am flight, then charter the same plane on to Chita, which seemed the better alternative at this point. Of course no one was available despite the promises made last night. Svieta, who was doing all the work - I only made the decisions - had to run between the Russian part of the airport terminal, the only available telephone, and me sitting patiently - or otherwise - on the baggage in the Intourist section. I was tired of trundling all the baggage around, and, for security reasons, watching everything very carefully because my 'money minder', Katie, who usually watched the one special bag which was our hidden 'bank', was far away with the others in the central team.

By 10.00 am I was thirsty. Because our overnight hostel had no restaurant, we had not even had a drink yet, so I went to the only place where we could get food. I ordered two sandwiches and some tea, then realising that Svieta would need feeding also, tried by sign language to indicate that I wanted two more. The woman waved me away. When I found Svieta and brought her in, she ordered for me, and I discovered that for reasons still unknown, the woman behind the counter would take no payment. Was it the miracles of Susuman still operating here?

With Svieta back I got the answer, "No!" To which of the many questions did this apply? "No", we could not charter the aircraft that would be flying into Blagoveshchensk; to charter on from there to Chita with them, the pilots would have to exceed their permitted number of flying hours. This was new to me in Russia, but at least it was an answer! Nonetheless we now tried desperately to join the queue for standby tickets for this flight, only to find that the last ones went to a man who rudely pushed his way past Svieta. Now we understood why we had not succeeded in chartering this plane, since we could not even get on it for the first leg! So now we only have one way to get out of this place today - no more flights, no more seats - but where is our man who last night offered us that charter for $18,000? He should have been here over an hour ago. Svieta had spoken to him on the phone, and he had said that despite our query over the price, he had provisionally scheduled the flight and we could be in the air by 10.00 am.

Suddenly he appeared, still assuring us that we could be in the air in an hour, still time to get to Chita for the Crusade, despite the fact that, in view of the length of the flight, we would have to go via Yakutsk to refuel. Yakutsk! I knew that Michael Krchnák was stranded in there with the team from Czechoslovakia. He had been calling our base at Chita for days saying that he could not get a flight out and he and the group would miss their return flight into Moscow. Yakutsk, more than any other, is a one-way town. We had got Michael's team in without difficulty, but there were definitely no flights out for two weeks!

Immediately as if by another miracle, I had the answer. I told Svieta to offer $14,000 provided that we flew via Yakutsk. He accepted subject to someone else he knew taking part charter with us. As we paid the money over and signed the agreement, I casually mentioned that we would be collecting another group of twelve at the refuelling stop in Yakutsk.

Our problem was again this demon that we battled against so many times in Siberia, the Zavtra spirit. 'Tomorrow!' Despite all the assurances and promises that we would be in Chita in plenty of time, by 2.00 pm even I, with all the faith I could muster, realised that we had problems. In my frustration I attempted to cancel, but found that it would cost me 50% of the price, the Czech group would still be marooned, and we would have no way at all to get to Chita.

You will understand now why when this whole Siberian Adventure was planned, right from the beginning it had been clearly understood by me that we needed our own aircraft! Either given, as we had hoped, by the German Government, or bought by ourselves, or as I had expected right up to the last moment before the Crusades began, at least our own charter aircraft to come with us all the way. The whole itinerary was virtually impossible without our own aircraft, but despite eight months or more of praying by our intercessors, the Lord had not answered in this way. Yet on reflection, probably our greatest miracles and the greatest demonstration of His power had been in the provision of the connecting flights. And this was no exception.

At 2.30 we were told to board the aircraft, but it was a farce. Even though we had our tickets in our hands, the woman at the boarding gate refused to accept us, saying that there was no flight scheduled to Chita. This lost us time. When a few frantic phone calls from her finally gave us clearance into the departure 'lounge', our official guide could not get us through the door on to the runway because it was locked and no one could find the key! Eventually they found a man who had the key all the time so at last by 3.00 we were actually loaded into the charter plane, a version of our favourite AN 24. This aircraft was identical except that it was a cargo plane. Whereas the AN 24 was designed for forty-eight passengers, this one, an AN 26, had a rear loading ramp and just hard plastic benches running the length of each side. No seat belts, nor it appeared any definite limit to the numbers who could travel. For the first time we saw that the other person on board was a woman sitting in a Lada Niva. We would be carrying her and the car to Chita. She didn't even get out of the car, but sat in it through the long hours in the air.

Now as I sat near the cockpit and watched the crew, I knew the procedure from our previous flights. But why don't they start the engines I thought? Svieta, sitting next to me, soon gave me the answer as she listened to their conversations with the control tower. They had not got clearance for take-off. Something to do either with the flight plan, or failure to complete some other documentation. They argued with the control tower, saying "Let us take off and we can sort this out later." What about the Zavtra spirit, I thought! Then it was OK, I saw the propellers begin to turn and I knew that we were going at last. Finally at 3.30 we taxied to the end of the runway and began accelerating for take-off.

These aircraft are designed for cargo, not passengers. We flew for three hours, it was deafeningly noisy, uncomfortable to speak except by shouting. No food, no drink. But if I turned right round the view from the window behind me was interesting. Svieta soon found a bench and lay down to try to sleep, but I just prayed, and watched as thousands of feet below me the panorama of Northern Siberia unfolded like a glorious picture being unrolled. Over the ground our speed was 300 mph., but up here in the blue sky, the forests, rivers, hills and lakes along with tiny houses, villages and towns passed by slowly. This was the Siberia of my vision, and everything God had promised WAS being fulfilled.

However, I began to dream as I saw in my mind next year's programme unfolding in panorama like the Siberian landscape below. I will return, this is the land to which God has called me and if necessary I will give my life just to bring the Glory of the Lord to cover this land, not with winter's snow, but Holy Spirit FIRE. This barren land - too cold for harvests - will yet yield another more wonderful harvest of souls. BUT I cannot reap without the tools. Right now Lord, find me my own airplane - just like this one, an AN 26. Please Father, turn my dream into a vision and the vision into reality.

As we drew closer to Yakutsk the view became more impressive, but I was now absorbed in asking God for a miracle that would speed up our journey - I desperately wanted to be in Chita for the meeting, or at least in time to pray for the sick. Please Lord, answer me once more! We landed at Yakutsk at 6.30 pm. Before we had left Magadan, Svieta had phoned through to Misha in Chita to tell him that we were indeed on our way and also to get in contact with Michael in Yakutsk urgently. We needed him to get his group to the airport to meet us.

Michael had received the call at about 10.00 am local time. Afterwards he told me that he had already spent about an hour and a half that morning really praying hard that he and the group would find some way of getting out. At that precise moment he received the call from Misha telling him to get everyone together and be at the airport by 2.00 pm - our original schedule. They dropped everything to get there. Meanwhile I had realised the problems they would have. Because we were a charter flight, his group would not be notified of our arrival and without tickets they would not be allowed to go through the process of checking themselves and their baggage through and getting to the boarding lounge.

The Lord was good to me as always. I asked my friends with whom I was chartering in Magadan to phone or radio through to Yakutsk to put out a call for Michael and the Czech group, to issue them with tickets, and have them waiting for me. Aeroflot for once excelled themselves, found the group in the airport building, issued tickets and had them already checked in and ready. The problem again was on the runway. I don't know why but the pilot seemed to have landed on the wrong spot. The crew got out and walked away from us, leaving just the mechanic to check the plane over. Time was passing and it took a full hour for them to finally get the fuel tanker up and fill the two main tanks of our thirsty flying machine. Next we watched expectantly as they brought a large catering truck alongside. For a moment I thought that we were going to have another miracle and get a meal. No, nothing like that, the truck travelled all that way just to bring some of Aeroflot's apology for lemonade! Only good if you are very thirsty, otherwise don't bother. Then finally a joyful re-union with Michael and his group who had arrived on an airport bus. There were not enough seats in the plane, even though there were only fourteen of us, but most of them sat on the floor or lay on their sleeping bags. Then as the engines burst into life we began the rush that would sweep the flying machine back into the blue sky and let it rest its wings on any light fluffy cloud it could find while its throbbing motors pulled the sky past the windows and resumed the task of unrolling the pictures below us.

In all it took us seven and a half hours flying time, plus the hour stopped. It must have been over 2,000 miles we flew that afternoon and evening. But to my great disappointment even allowing for the three hour time change in our favour, it was 9.00 pm when I saw the lights of Chita coming into view and in the dusk I recognised familiar landmarks as the aircraft took a wide turn and descended on to the gravel of the still unfinished runway. Misha was pleased to welcome us once again. We had a large team gathered in the town because tomorrow was the 'March for Jesus'. This meant there were fortunately plenty of others to speak in the stadium in my absence and in the end it was Gary who was chosen. There had been a good response to the appeal. But I had rescued the Czech team, and I was here for the March and the two remaining nights of the Crusade.

This was the last meeting I missed here in Siberia. In nine weeks I missed only four opening nights, and it was a great miracle and testimony to God that I got into and out of every city. With lesser faith and a lesser God I would not even have tried!

Chapter 14

CHITA - WHERE THE DEMON SPOKE TO ME

I had arrived in Chita very late Friday night. Both Svieta and I were tired. But who could resist Misha's excitement? "This morning is our March for Jesus! You must come!" In the West we sometimes forget what it means for a Russian to march freely through the streets of his town, proclaiming the Name of Jesus, and this was their first public march in Chita.

When we got to the rendezvous we found a vast crowd already gathered from Misha's church, but also our Team A under Richard's leadership and the remnant of Team C who had so unfortunately been expelled from the south-east region after their crusade in Amursk. In addition there were the whole of our Czech team who had just flown in with me from Yakutsk under the leadership of Michael Krchnák, some of our Bulgarian and Hungarian helpers, and also Pastor Heinrich Buller from Augsburg, Germany along with members of his church and family. Our teams had got heavily involved in the preparation of banners which proclaimed the Lordship of Jesus in English, Russian, German, Hungarian and Czech - one God, one message of love from many different nations, one Body of Christ.

So with banners waving, accompanied by a truck with amplifiers and music, the group marched into the city centre. We ended up in Victory Square under a huge bellicose monument, but today we were celebrating Christ's Victory over years of Christian persecution and repression. People from the nearby market stalls flocked to hear the song of the Lord. How pleasing it must have sounded to His ears, coming from this land that had so long rejected Him! The local church music group sang, our group from the central team sang, singers and pantomime artistes from Team A performed, and Heinrich's people sang in Russian, English, German and Hebrew till they had the whole crowd dancing for joy to their lovely music.

I went into the Chita stadium on that Saturday night on fire for God, touched by all the miracles I had seen Him perform here in Siberia, touched by His love. I said:

> God loves us, but the real miracle happens when we love God. I have such a great love for Russia in my heart, and God loves you. God made everything perfect. What went wrong? It was the devil who made men sin. Sickness doesn't come from God. The suffering in Magadan and Susuman doesn't come from God. He loves them, He loves Chita, He loves all Russia, He wants to set you free. Siberia is burning into my heart because God has seen the suffering of Siberia, the blood of the innocent - this land is stained by the blood of millions of innocent people. But God is a God of love, forgiveness and power. He will pour out greater blessing on Siberia than on any other nation in the world. He says, "I will heal your land, I will heal your people." Because God made us and loves us and is our Father, He sent Jesus to reach out to us, to visit us in our shame and suffering, to cleanse THIS land. The New Testament is the best love story in the world, and I have come with a prophetic message from God to you - you will never know how much it has cost me to get here. But Jesus loved you so much He came to pay the price of sin (there is no punishment if you believe in Him); He came to take

away your sickness (everyone who touched Jesus was healed); He came to break the power of Satan (to set you free here in Chita). Have faith in Christ, and that faith will change the whole direction of your life NOW, like the lieutenant in Susuman who had a bullet through his leg and ankle. When he believed he was instantly healed and ran! But not just his body - his whole life was changed. If you will really believe in Jesus tonight, He'll forgive your sin, heal your body, change your life!

The people were so convicted by this message that once again it appeared every unbeliever came forward and once again there was a terrific crush for healing. I will only select two that made an impression on me. A middle-aged woman in a green outfit stood in front of me. She took the hairpin out of her bun, shook her blonde hair down and revealed a cumbersome hearing-aid she had so cleverly hidden. We prayed. Someone called her name and spoke to her from the crowd. To her delight, she could hear every word! Next a mother held up her little boy to us. Through Svieta she told us he had sight problems so severe, no one could help. I looked at the mother who herself was wearing bottle-thick glasses. Her sight had failed as the result of an illness when she was only seven years old. I prayed, and she could see! Then her little son suddenly saw - he spotted his grandmother in the distance! Then his older sister who was with them also received her sight, and could read all the letters on the usher's badge. The whole family came again the next day - without their glasses of course!

On the Sunday, I preached in the church Misha co-pastored with Andrei. This was the very place where, a year before, I had had the most extraordinary encounter with a ruling demon. We had found Chita to be a city without God, only one Spirit-filled Church for 400,000 people, its only monuments, raised like gods on their pedestals, were tanks, soldiers with guns, space rockets and of course, in the centre, Lenin himself. The last cathedral was dynamited in 1937 to make way for his statue. We were told that the city was founded on the death and suffering of the martyrs 150 years ago, being originally built to house the exiled prisoners from the Czarist government. Because of the extreme conditions - working in mines - and the cold, minus 45-50 degrees centigrade in winter, and lack of food, thousands died. As elsewhere in Siberia, even the roads we drove over were laid on the bones of the prisoners who died in great suffering, many of them believers exiled from European Russia. Until three years ago Chita was, like many others in Siberia, a totally closed city - no foreigners, not even Russians, were allowed in. We were the first British evangelists ever to enter the city. Half the population was military, the other half seemed to be exiles and their families. It was here last year, in Misha and Andrei's church in the local Culture House that the Holy Spirit brought me face to face with the controlling demon of Russia. We had held a three day crusade in the stadium but returning to the church on the Saturday night, Misha had told me of the strong demonic presence which had hindered every service since they had moved into the Culture House.

Before the meeting I joined the church intercessors backstage in spiritual warfare. After an hour the intercessors left to begin the meeting. The Holy Spirit prompted me to stay on, then led me to go behind the back curtain on the stage.

In the darkness I saw a demonic figure with green fire in its eyes, which began to talk to me. I now know that it was a bust of Lenin on a pedestal six feet in height which faced me, but at that moment the demon spoke clearly. It told me that it was the son of Lucifer and boasted. "I was in Lenin and everyone thinks that I am dead, but I still live on and I am the spirit controlling Russia today!"

I took authority in the Name of Jesus, breaking its power and touching its forehead symbolically as if with the Blood of Christ. Again I warned this demon that his power was broken and that I came in the Name of the One stronger than him, that in that Name of Jesus I would take the whole of Russia for Christ. Finally I bound him and took authority over him.

From that moment the demonic curse in the building was broken. I prophesied that to demonstrate this, when we saw Lenin's body taken from the Mausoleum in Red Square and buried, this spirit's power would be gone for ever.

After that there was indeed a new freedom to preach and to minister the Gospel in that place. Returning one year later, I found a lifeless Lenin still there - he was after all the property of the local authority and therefore had not been destroyed - but his once extraordinary eyes were now quite powerless. Now it was here that I was to give one of my most powerful messages to Siberia.

I have a vision so strong it burns in my heart, but it is not just to evangelise. Since I have been here in your country ten Crusades have gone, this is the eleventh and there are six more to go. But this is only the beginning of what God wants to do in Siberia. Evangelism is only opening a door and I will not let go of God till He does what He's promised in this nation. If only you could see what I see, know what I know. I know the suffering of your people, that for seven hundred years the devil has controlled this land. The spirit of antichrist entered Russia through Chita in the person of Genghis Khan. But his power is broken. Jesus is Lord! Now! Today!

God is speaking prophetically over the whole of this nation. He will fulfil His vision. In Ezekiel Chapter 12 starting at verse 21, God rebuked the prophets, the people of Israel, the Church, for saying, "Every vision fails."

God says, "I will make this proverb cease. The fulfilment of every vision is at hand!" God is saying all the visions about Russia will be fulfilled, the day has now come - not the future - now! Today!

But the people didn't believe the prophet that the vision is for today. They said in verse 27, "He prophesies about what is a long way off." God has burned verse 28 in my heart, His answer, "None of My Words shall be delayed any more. The Word I have spoken shall be done." There is no more delay. God will now fulfil every word He has given. This is why God has sent me here. To evangelise, to open churches, to work miracles is only the beginning here in Siberia.

Suddenly the Power of God will come down, greater than Pentecost, and when this second Pentecost comes, the whole world will see the Glory of God. Jesus is coming soon, but before, God is going to exalt the Name of Jesus in the whole earth by miracles, by signs and wonders so great the eyes of the whole world will look and say "It's impossible, it must be God!" The vision burns within me. There is one nation above all others where God is going to show His Glory and Power - not only Israel - but God has chosen Siberia and Russia, at this moment in time, as the place where He is going to pour out the Power of the Holy Spirit. I have come at the call of God.

God has chosen this nation for many reasons, partly because of its prophetic connection with Israel *(Ezekiel 38 and 39)*, partly because Satan has chosen this land, but God has broken his power. Let us rejoice God has chosen this nation above all the nations, a nation that has denied God, where the Bible has been destroyed and Christians persecuted. More blood has been shed in Siberia than in

any other part of the world, and the blood of the martyrs
cries out to God. God will answer and great Revival WILL
come here. This land WILL see the Glory of God. I know
it so strongly. I seek God for the fulfilment of this vision,
and I will tell you how you can be part of the fulfilment.

There are two ways God will fulfil the Words He has
spoken. Firstly, through faith. Numbers Chapter 13
shows us the children of Israel at the very gateway of the
land they were to possess. God speaks to you, the Church,
today. He has opened up a tremendous vision of what He
wants to do, a second Pentecost here in this nation that has
despised Jesus above every other nation - this is the nation
that has defiled the Name of Jesus and said that God is
dead. BUT YOU ARE ON THE EDGE OF THE
FULFILMENT OF WHAT GOD IS GOING TO DO.
Israel in Numbers Chapter 13 stood in the same place -
they stood within days, hours of the fulfilment of all that
God and the prophets had spoken.

Twelve spies were sent into the land to see and experience
the vision. They saw all that God had promised was true.
All they had to do was to get up and take it by faith. They
ALL saw it. God hadn't failed. Two saw no problem, ten
saw all the problems - big cities, fortified armies, giants.
"We can't," they said and they told the people not to go.
Two said, "We can do it in the Power of God - our God is
with us - we can overcome every obstacle."

Who did the people believe? They only believed those
who said God can't do it. They didn't believe the men who
believed.

God WILL set this land free from the curse, the evil.
Nothing is impossible with God. Lift up the Name of

Jesus! All things are possible. Rise up in the Name of Jesus! *(At this point the entire congregation stood to their feet.)*

We're going to follow, not Moses, but Jesus. We're going to take this land by the Power of the Holy Ghost. That's why God has called me here, to speak to you as a prophet. "I have a vision for Magadan from Ezekiel Chapter 37, the valley of dry bones. Thousands upon thousands of dead men. You know the death camps, the suffering under Stalin - the whole land around that town is stained red with blood, many were believers. Nothing is impossible. God can take the believers who died for their faith in Magadan. He can open their graves to preach the Gospel. If you won't do it, if you won't receive the Spirit and Power of God, God WILL raise the dead to preach the Gospel in this land.

God has shown me what He can do. If you could see what I see, know the God that I know, you would know what God will do in Russia. God loves Russia and He will save this nation.

If you want to be part of the fulfilment of this vision, you must first believe God. Second, you must obey Him. The Bible is full of what Abraham DID by faith. Hebrews Chapter 11 verse 8 tells us Abraham 'obeyed and went, not knowing'. Abraham believed God so much that, though he lived in prosperity, he left everything. He only knew God had said, "Go!", but he loved God with such power and such intensity that he went. God will move in our lives when we have that same faith. God is calling us - we must obey - this is more and better than sacrifice. Get out and do what God says. There's a world out there that needs Jesus. I don't know where you're going, but get up and go! Do it!

People talk to me about faith. If you believe God, your life will change, you'll DO something. I believe God. I can't stay in England. I'm here because, like Abraham, I believe God. God never makes mistakes. He works miracles through our faith in Him. You've all got faith! But First Corinthians Chapter 12 tells us there is a gift of faith that comes through the power of the Holy Spirit. Ask for this faith, faith to believe God, faith to get up and go. This faith is only given to those who obey God. No obedience, no gift of faith.

Russia WILL have Revival. Here in Chita - today - the Fire of God is coming down. I have more power of the Holy Spirit in my life now than ever before. The promise is for today! Now!

Pray! Pray till you get power with God!

The Power of God fell on that packed Church, followed by weeping and supplication and prayer to God for Russia to be saved. Back in the apartment where I was staying, I continued to pray on my own. God added this solemn warning to the morning's message:

"Beware therefore lest what has been spoken by the prophets come upon you, 'Behold you despisers, marvel and perish' - for I work a work in your days, a work which you will by no means believe, though one were to declare it to you." Acts 13:40-41.

Later that afternoon I was fetched from the apartment by car. As we drove down the avenue leading to the stadium we passed a long column of soldiers in uniform, marching two by two, military fashion, in the same direction. A civilian and an officer were leading them. I commented how wonderful it would be if they were heading for the meeting! Shortly after our own arrival, there was a sudden stir in the crowd, people began turning to look, and burst out clapping! Imagine my joy - the entire formation was winding into the stadium and filling up one complete section of seats. There must have been more than three hundred soldiers there. We learned afterwards that they had been brought in by their captain who had given his life to the Lord at the Friday night meeting!

The most thrilling thing was that when I made the appeal for a decision for Christ, every single soldier came forward for salvation, including others who were scattered among the rest of the crowd. But please do not think they came forward out of a sense of duty, one following the other. Our cameraman filmed them reaching out to get their New Testaments. He said never had he seen any as hungry for the Word of God as these men were. They literally fought and struggled to get their copies.

It was our policy to give a New Testament to all the new converts in Siberia. Originally the proposal was only to give a Gospel of John, but we realised that most of these people would never be able to buy a Bible so we made a decision to give at least a New Testament. We had anticipated a cost of approximately £1 each to print and deliver them to Siberia. Amongst the many other good things which Misha had done as well as organising the Crusades for us, was to obtain these New Testaments. On one of his visits to meet me in Germany with Heinrich Buller, Misha had seen an opportunity to purchase New Testaments in Moscow. He had been offered 100,000 for only 17,000 DM inclusive of delivery to Siberia. This was the equivalent of about £7,000, or only 7p each copy.

Time was short, he was returning to Siberia via Moscow within three days. I had put this wonderful proposition before our friends and supporters in Germany, who responded sacrificially by raising the whole amount in time for Misha to take back to Moscow with him. Immediately God responded to the sacrifice and in Moscow Misha was able to obtain not one but two hundred thousand New Testaments for this same price, thus making it only 3.5p each. In addition they gave him a two ton container of Russian tracts free, which meant that our teams doing street evangelism had the tracts they really needed to distribute.

We saw some wonderful healings that Sunday afternoon in Chita, but I will focus on just two. The first was an old man, walking with a stick, paralysed on his left side. He was healed, and I led him to the platform to testify and give glory to God through the microphone. But he danced and danced! The second was also a lovely story, a young man Pastor Sergei had brought all the way up from Duldurga, a five hour journey away. This young man lived twelve kilometres outside that small town, and he had found no-one to take him to the meetings when I was there a few weeks before. But he was convinced, if only he could get to the Crusade in Chita, God would heal him.

His problem was he had been in a motorbike accident. His right leg was now paralysed, a full 5 cm shorter than his other leg, his knee firmly locked and his foot twisted and turned inwards. He could only hop with crutches with great difficulty because of the enormous strain on the rest of his body. He had stood expectantly throughout the service, propped up against the barrier, determined to be first in the queue. When I prayed, there was a small improvement. I asked him to sit down and wait a while. During this time his faith was built up as more and more people were healed. When I went back to him, his leg grew out significantly, then his right ankle straightened and strengthened. Then the pain left both his legs. But what he wanted so much was for his locked knee to bend. Finally it began to loosen. Now he had two matching legs! He was fully satisfied and thrust away his crutches most emphatically. He had finally got what he wanted! Phil, our cameraman, ran after him with the crutches to take a picture, but he absolutely refused to touch those things again, not even for a photograph - he was so triumphant and rejoicing in what God had done!

Chapter 15

UST KUT - WE ONLY HAD 30 HOURS

Before leaving Chita it was important for me to meet with the deputy mayoress of the city, Mrs Kim whom I knew well from my previous visit eighteen months before. The contact had been very productive and established a very good relationship with the city. One of the things that had emerged from the conversation was that they urgently needed a second electric power generating station. This would supply the whole Chita region with power for the factories and businesses as well as the private homes. As a by-product the waste heat from the power plant would provide extra heating for the big apartment blocks where most people lived, which was a desperate need for the winter. Lack of power meant a system of rationing, both for power and heating as well as insufficient power to develop the manufacturing industry on which the city was dependent for employment.

Having had correspondence during the year from her, Mrs Kim was again anxious to meet me and during a very fruitful meeting I was able to indicate that some progress was being made to get the power station installed. Mrs Kim and Misha both pointed out that if we could actually do something to help, the whole region would be very grateful to us. Potentially this could open up the whole area as never before to the Gospel and we could have the support of the city authorities! This city is very important to us strategically, because here Misha is co-pastor of the largest church in Siberia, and we are establishing our mission base here in this city.

We left Chita, where we have so many friends, with reluctance. I know that I will be back here again many times, my heart is right here amongst these people.

Misha took us to the airport for the 9.30 am flight to Ust Kut believing that our tickets had been reserved for us in advance. This was being organised by a man at the airport who was Misha's friend, and who had been responsible for helping us so much in the past. Unfortunately this man was away on holiday and nothing had been done. This meant that once again we had no possibility of getting on to the flight which we had expected. Now Misha had a real problem, his only way to get us to Ust Kut in time for the Crusade was to charter a plane and get it organised quickly. It was the usual story of the inability to get any action here in Russia with this Zavtra spirit. Finally we took to the air at 4.00 pm in the afternoon, but even with the gain of one hour through the time change, the AN 24 did not land at Ust Kut until 5.00 pm. This would have been all right except that the Crusade was due to start at 6.00 pm. It was a great blessing therefore to find that the Pastor was already waiting for us as the aircraft rolled to a standstill.

Rick Bettles, who looked after the sound system for me throughout the nine weeks in Siberia, did not like the look of the large dumper truck which had been hired by the local church. Normally used to transport stone, the vehicle did not have suitable suspension to carry the precious and very delicate equipment, which had already been battered by all the travel, but there was no alternative. Quickly loading everything into the truck, the sound system and all our baggage, Rick, Yura from Kiev and some of the others climbed in to try to make sure that no more harm would come to it.

Our men on the central team who handled the two tons of equipment almost daily did a sterling job. Rick who took overall responsibility had come as intercessor and sound engineer; Phil, our cameraman, also assisted him throughout; Gary, from one of our ground teams, was co-opted for his strength and size part-way through the crusades. They could not have managed without the help of Roma from the music group and Yura, Rick's special assistant, only seventeen years old and an ex-heavy metal drummer, who was later to become sole sound engineer for our Ukrainian crusades. On this occasion they found that the best way was for them to travel in the back of the big uncomfortable truck, crouched down so that the police would not see them! They rode like this all the way to the stadium while Svieta and I and the rest travelled in comparative luxury in the comfort of the Pastor's Lada.

In this very hurried manner, we arrived first and watched as the big, dirty truck followed us into the large stadium, literally with five minutes to spare before the service should start. Already the place was full and crowds were still streaming in; that meant that there was no time to wash and change, no possibility to get any food or drink - these people needed Christ! Our job was to preach the Gospel. All I had time to do was to get one of the men to find my bag on the back of the truck. This way I managed to get out a clean shirt and look for a store room under the stands where I changed. Still there was no food or drink, despite the fact that we had eaten nothing since breakfast. So I sent someone out to a shop and he came back with a bottle of lemonade - that is all we had!

It only took Rick ten minutes with help from Yura and Phil to connect up the sound system so that the girls with Roma in the praise and worship team could start ministering. This at least would give me forty minutes to collect my thoughts, pray, and get ready to speak.

The response was wonderful. To see about 3000 stream

forward onto the grass of the field in front of me to accept Christ was enough reward after the struggle to get there. Yes it was tough; never before going to Siberia had I ever faced such actual physical hardship in obeying God's call to preach the Gospel. Still, if this was the only way, I would do it again gladly, in order to see so many find Christ. The price we would pay in Siberia is nothing compared to what physical price Jesus paid to win our salvation.

Then our joy was increased as we witnessed the miracles of healing which came as I prayed with the sick. Looking back I see from the records that there was a tremendous anointing that night. Katie identified more than thirty-five different people whose healings, amongst the hundreds that were delivered, were outstanding instant miracles.

After the service had finished late that night, it was a special relief to be driven by car to an apartment where I had some 'chai' but was too tired to eat. I fell into bed, wearied but rejoicing. God has blessed me with an ability to simply commit all the problems to him, then just fall asleep. I sometimes wonder whether it is out of faith - or sheer exhaustion!

The next morning I was awake early and after a good Russian style breakfast, went to the local church at 9.00 am, to meet the ground team for prayer. Some of the central team joined me and together we had a very powerful time of praise and worship followed by intercession and prayer for the Crusade. These hours spent together with our group and others from the local church fellowship are so important in bringing the blessing of God into these Crusades.

After this meeting I spent some time with Yuri, the Pastor of the local church who were supporting and helping to organise the whole of the evangelism in the area with us. He said that he had come from the Black Sea area of the Ukraine with his wife only three years ago to found this church. God had put such a love in his heart for Siberia, that as he said, "I must sacrifice myself here for God." He meant this because he was very much alone, even in this Baikal region. There was no other church he could fellowship with for at least 250 miles East or West, and as much as 600 miles North or South. His work has been so blessed by the Lord that now he has opened three other smaller churches, but he has many problems caused simply because all the believers are so new in Christ. One of the new churches is nine hours travelling away and the man pastoring it was the first man to be baptised by Yuri after he came here. However, they have a real challenge to spiritual warfare, because there is a satanist church in the same place.

Since arriving in Ust Kut, I have had to deal constantly with problems within the ground team who came here a week in advance, to do the street evangelism. It is not easy even for our people to work here because of the demonic opposition, so I can understand the Pastor's situation. With our own group my thought is, if only they would not bring all their problems to me the moment I arrive! Katie and Svieta were becoming very concerned over this. Even though I had arrived with so little time before the Crusade last night, they still needed to burden me before the meeting started, while I wanted to spend time in prayer with the Lord before speaking. Thank God however, that after the prayer time this morning things have been resolved.

I also have to sort out the payment of all the bills for the ground team and organise their transportation to the next Crusade myself. It is becoming very obvious that I have no one in my central team to take some of this burden off me. I sense the pressure building up, and I need to get more men around me who can support. It is enough to have all the travelling and to preach every meeting, without all the other organisational matters. But Siberia is not like the rest of Europe, it takes a great deal of organisational skill as well as more faith than I have ever needed before to handle these problems. Only now do I see the years of preparation and training God has had to give me to equip me for this moment. My experience of running my own travel company for many years is invaluable, but even this did not prepare me for my 'Siberian Adventure'. Who can I find who will really stand with me? I thank God daily for the prompting to bring four intercessors with me on this central team. They pray constantly for the problems and difficulties which arise by the minute and need on the spot attention. No time to contact those other intercessors who are praying constantly on a twenty-four hour, round-the-clock basis. I had believed that amongst the four with me would be an Aaron and a Hur to hold up my arms like they did for Moses. However this needs great sacrifice and God will provide. Here in Siberia all of us are coming under the attack of the devil. I feel that the anointing on me is growing stronger, but the devil is also getting madder! However the victory is already ours in Christ, the devil is already defeated, we just need to take the authority which is ours in Christ and tell the devil constantly that his power is broken.

That night we went to the stadium for the second Crusade meeting in Ust Kut. The news of all the miracles that had happened the night before has spread like wildfire. Tonight, over 4000 pack into the stands and overflow on to the grass. After speaking, as I invite them to accept Christ the whole crowd stream forward, only a few believers are left still sitting. We need all the men from the local church to assist the forty people in our ground team to prevent the excited crowds pressing forward. Unless we stop them, they will trample on the cables running between the speakers, the mixer desk, and the amplifiers and damage all our equipment. This was always a worry to Rick.

If the people are excited now, they will become more so when I start to pray for the sick! In their haste and determination to be healed, they will stop at nothing, especially a thin line of British men and women unused to having to physically restrain desperate people from all being healed at once. I still laugh at the memories of those sweet little old 'babushkas,' fighting with feet and elbows as well as sticks and crutches, to get in front of me and attract my attention so that they can be delivered from all their pain and suffering. They really know that there is no hope from doctors; either they have been to hospital and ended up worse, or they are just too old and the system will not help them. Having been into so many of the Russian hospitals, I am aware of the poor and antiquated equipment, the lack of suitable drugs and medicines, as well as the total lack of finance which means dirty linen and dilapidated facilities.

Now the power of God began to move over the sick, a very great sense of the power of God present to heal. One of the first was a young man who had been brought out of the hospital especially for prayer. He was in such great pain because he had been hit and run over by a motorbike. His spine was broken and he had severe internal injuries, yet as I laid my hands on him he was completely healed and, totally freed from pain, could bend his back without difficulty. The next was a little boy who had also had an accident. He had a lump on his spine and his legs were weak and could not hold him. Totally healed, even the lump on his spine went. Also healed was a little girl who had pain in her back and legs. Then we prayed for a whole group of deaf and dumb children who all got healed so that they could both hear and speak.

This night I had to leave the Crusade meeting early before it had finally finished, but the others went on praying and many more miracles happened. I went as quickly as possible back to the apartment where I had been staying for a meal, then went down to the railway station to try to get tickets so that the whole of the central team could get on to the midnight train to Bratsk. I had only been in the town of Ust Kut for thirty hours, during which time I had held two Crusade meetings and seen nearly 7,000 come to

Christ, but could not stay any longer.

The only way to get out of the town that night was by train. We had in front of us the longest and most difficult journey of all so far, over 2000 miles across the total width of the territory which we were covering, from West of Lake Baikal right to the Far East, facing the Kamchatka peninsular, almost at the Pacific Ocean, in order to make the next Crusade in Sovietskaya Gavan.

There were no night flights out of Ust Kut, but because of the time factor, we dared not delay our departure. However the Pastor we would later work with in Bratsk who had come with his family to support us in Ust Kut, had told us that a member of his church worked in the airport at Bratsk and would get us tickets early next morning for the first part of our journey to Sovietskaya. Our immediate problem now was that there were no tickets left for this overnight train, quite normal in these parts! To help us, a member of the local church had gone in advance to the station with a lot of my money in his pocket. He had convinced me that there was a way to get the twelve of us now left in the central team on to the train that night.

We needed a lot of trust, first this man had my money! Then secondly, he said that he knew someone, who knew someone who knew the guard on the train. Standing in the dark on the platform with the train seemingly impatient to shake, rattle and roll its way into the forbidding, unknown distance, with the responsibility for twelve people and about two tons of baggage, not certain if we have tickets or not, or if we have, which of the twenty carriages would be the one chosen to shelter us in its gloomy, unwelcoming interior - all this was awesome! Anyway where was the man with my money? By now we realised that no one knew where he was, or in the dark, who he was! Some confusion ensued when two different people shouted out different carriage numbers, but somehow we had to load everything quickly, tickets or not! Which we did, trying to make sure that all the luggage as well as all the gear went on. None of us had less than two bags each, some it seemed had an innumerable number, one bag according to rumour carried the famous 'Baikal Rock Collection,' as well as clothing. Being Ukrainian, Svetlana never understood that English joke.

Before I had time to check thoroughly, the train was already moving, so the Ukrainians, who always seemed to understand how this confusion worked, took some more of my fast depleting finances and went to find the bedding for our bunks. Later we found out how the system of getting non-existent tickets operates. The guards seem to have developed a method of remembering at the last minute which seats have not been sold, then like this they sell them rather profitably, to those who like us, are desperate to travel, usually, (but not on this occasion), at a very inflated price.

So it was that we arrived, tired, but expectantly at 7.00 am next morning at the station in Bratsk and hired a number of taxis to get us to the airport. No problem, God had prepared the way in answer to prayer, tickets were available from the church member in the office, and we caught the flight direct into Khabarovsk, arriving early afternoon because of the time change. How easy it was!

It was our sixth time through Khabarovsk and we had decided not to bother the local Pastor, just to manage on our own, because his car had collapsed and was beyond repair. With Svetlana's help we took a taxi to the town and the Aeroflot office. This time Phil came out with us to film for the record all our struggles with Aeroflot. Despite all promises given in advance, there were no tickets available for the next leg of the journey into Sovietskaya Gavan. We tried desperately in two different offices without avail.

Not being able to achieve this we could however, and did,

reserve tickets for the flight next week on our return from Sovietskaya Gavan, for the 11.00 am flight on the Monday, up to the next Crusade in Neryungri. But this did not get us tickets either into or out of the Crusade which would begin tomorrow in Sovietskaya Gavan. We tried to get train tickets, but although there was one leaving at 6.40 pm it took 36 hours, and would not reach in time for the Crusade which would start in only 24 hours.

It was a long time before we returned to our group who were still waiting with incredible patience, sitting on the baggage in the airport. Our only chance was to try the smaller airport opposite the main one, and charter from them. It was late now, but there was one woman available who offered us an aircraft for the following morning at a very reasonable price. We also found the 'Airport Hotel' next to this small airfield, so moved everything to it, and booked ourselves the usual two rooms for the night.

Having been all day without food as so often happened when travelling, I then took the group and we traipsed back to the larger airport in search of sustenance. Actually the main airport at Khabarovsk had four buildings. On the right was a big new building used by the Russian nationals only. We were segregated at these airports, usually the nationals used vastly inferior facilities, while we had to go into the so-called 'Intourist' building. As our central team was half British and half Ukrainians, we sometimes had to separate at check-in. Ukrainians were classed as Russian and travelled at approximately half our 'Intourist' fare. Where possible we found favour and managed to travel with them at 'Russian' prices. This also meant that we could then all go to the same place and check-in together. Otherwise, as in Khabarovsk, we British had to buy our tickets and go through the 'Intourist' side. This was old, in primitive condition, housed in a smaller, but rather grand and ornate building to the left. In the middle was the worst section, the arrivals area for Westerner and Russian alike. Small and crowded, with no room to move, the roof let in water, the only way in from the runway being through a corrugated iron corridor where the rain poured in, soaking the floor. There was never room to put all our gear when we collected it from the aircraft and hauled it piece by piece into this congested space, let alone room for any other arriving passengers and relatives waiting for them. It made no difference on our seven visits here whether by scheduled flight or charter, we always had to use this way in.

The fourth building on the far left was a very special new airport terminal built by the Japanese who have conspicuously begun to invade this region. It was beautiful, containing a bank where we got the best exchange rate for our dollars against the rouble, spotlessly clean with 'western type' toilets, telephones and even clean, modern restaurants - when they were open! The Japanese charged a fee of at least $30 per person tax to all passengers who used it. Unfortunately no internal flights went from here, only to and from North America and Japan, which meant that all we could ever do was to gaze at it enviously and use the toilets! However, now I was able to treat the group to an evening meal here. In typical Russian style, the restaurant was closed and even the alternative Italian style place had to be persuaded to serve anything.

Next morning we all had been told to be at the small airport near our hotel by 8.00 am to check in for our flight. Last night before going to bed I had taken some of the men to see the airplanes, especially the one which we thought we were going to charter. The woman with whom I had spoken had quoted me only just over 2,000 dollars for an aircraft which was smaller than the AN 24 we were familiar with, but looking at it, the plane was modern and looked plenty big enough.

This is not what greeted me next morning. Going into the office, I had to meet the airport director and I remembered him from a previous time when he had bluntly refused to charter a plane to us. So I was somewhat apprehensive, especially when he said that the plane we had expected to charter was too small. He said that we needed a larger one, an AN 28, a new one to me. Also he said that the price quoted to me last night by the woman upstairs was incorrect. She had ignorantly quoted the price for Russians; as Westerners we must pay more. We had to understand that the Russians were poor and paid lower prices and that we were the rich capitalists who could afford to subsidise the whole Russian economy! I argued and tried everything but he was adamant. He could not care whether we had the aircraft or not, he was rude, abrupt and unwilling to communicate much except "niet!" Realising that time was short and that we had to get urgently to Sovietskaya Gavan because the first Crusade meeting was tonight, also that there were no possible alternatives, I eventually agreed to pay double the previous night's price, otherwise, the airport director said, there would be no aircraft available for us. And that meant no Crusade.

Now we had the tortuous task of bringing all the equipment and baggage five or six hundred yards by ourselves into the check-in. Everything was weighed piece by piece. Then to our horror, the large 'babushka' who was dealing with us said that we were 200 kg overweight! This despite the long arguments about weight which I thought I had settled with the airport director who had decided on this aircraft. Either we leave 200 kg of equipment or three persons, or ...! Looking at the largest member of the group, Gary Moore, I chose him and, for convenience, another young man with him, plus unnecessary bits of equipment, like sets of wheels which the Ukrainians and I used for moving our baggage. We then had to weigh Gary, Yura and all the bits. They came to exactly 200 kg. We could make it now.

This sorted, we loaded everything on the plane. Now only ten of us in number, we climbed on board this small AN 28 for the ninety minute flight to Sovietskaya Gavan. After everything had been loaded, the 'babushka' who had calculated all the weight with only the aid of her pencil and a scrap of paper, now decided that she had made a mistake in the calculation and that we were now under weight, then she decided that we weren't! Could she add up or not? If not, was the aircraft still overloaded and would it simply fail to lift off the runway, or after take-off would it slowly sink back down to the ground halfway? No, my faith is stronger than that, my apprehension was being reserved for problems on our arrival in Sovietskaya Gavan.

Chapter 16

SOVIETSKAYA GAVAN - THE PROPHECY WAS FULFILLED

We should have had a ground team in Sovietskaya Gavan seven days in advance, but the team in question, C Team, had been expelled from Amursk because of problems and we had had to disband them. They had been told by the police that their visas made out for Chita were not in order. It is true that Chita was to have been the base camp into which all the incoming groups whether from England or from the Ukraine would first go on arrival in Siberia. From there we would divide them into five separate teams and distribute them to cover the seventeen Crusades. The visas obtained in advance stated only Chita, because until the individual members arrived in Siberia we could not accurately determine which towns they would finally be sent on to. However, at the last minute, due to the closure of the airport at Chita, our base camp had been re-sited at Ulan Ude. This meant that none of this group had had their visas stamped in Chita. At least this was the reason the police gave, fining them about $2 each.

The real difficulty was that in this area the authorities were objecting to street evangelism and because of the team's activities, the police were looking for an excuse to expel them and not allow them anywhere within the region. This meant that they could not go to their next Crusade at Sovietskaya Gavan. Two Germans however who were part of the multinational team did not have this problem and had been able to go on, followed by two others from the central team who had volunteered to do the preparation for us.

As the AN 28 landed it taxied to the far end of the runway where there was an airport bus obligingly waiting for us to unload and carry everything aboard for the ride to the terminal building. In vain we, in the now rather depleted central team, looked for some sign of the ground team or the local pastor who had always up till now welcomed us into the town. Absolutely no one anywhere in sight, and the airport as usual was about an hour's drive from the town. To make matters worse, we had all the equipment with us, two of our baggage-carrying men were left behind in Khabarovsk and there were no taxis even! Worse still we discovered that there were two towns in the area, both an hour away in opposite directions and we suddenly realised we had no idea which one the stadium was in! Our German helpers, whom we had been contacting by phone, were staying in the other town, not Sovietskaya and this was now beginning to confuse us.

We sat for one hour then two, praying that someone would come. By now it was 2.00 pm and we needed to get all the equipment set up, as well as having a meal, a wash and change of clothes. Remember that we had had no breakfast and that there never was any food or drink on the planes.

All I wanted to do was to relax and let my ground team take over. I would need all my strength in a few hours to get up and preach the Gospel and heal the sick, there would be no time for rest.

But where were our ground team? We had waited two hours in the heat, I was physically and spiritually exhausted after my two day battle to get here, with little food or sleep to refresh me. I understood now how often Jesus must have been wearied by discouragement as well as tiredness. I was discouraged and tired, so near, yet so far. Then some of the intercessors who saw my real need, gathered round and began to pray for me.

So often in the stadium they saw me so bold and strong, defying the devil, delivering the lost from the threat of hell and the sick from the power of Satan. So many times they had seen me facing the totally impossible and taking authority by the power of Jesus' Name, demonstrating miracles of the supernatural by faith in Him. Daily defying the devil, always able to take the victory by faith. Look at all the miracles we have seen so far! Yet like Jesus, I too can have moments of tiredness, and so desperately need support and encouragement.

Suddenly the first breakthrough. A man sitting near me began to talk to us. He was an American businessman waiting for the next flight out, having been defeated in a major business deal, trying to buy almost new Russian warships for scrap. He recognised me, ''I've seen your picture on a poster in my hotel,'' he said. ''You're here for this Crusade in the stadium aren't you?'' ''Yes,'' I answered, ''but tell me where is the stadium?!''

It was such a relief to know that the publicity had been so well done in the town that this businessman knew about the Crusade and had recognised me, and knew the exact place we should go. Then one of the Ukrainian girls rushed in to tell us that there was an airport bus going to the correct town, and it was waiting outside. Loading everything inside the bus was no problem to us, although heavy work, but it was a problem to the driver and the passengers because we commandeered all the available seats! However the bus took us directly to the stadium and dropped us outside. All the equipment, all our baggage and ten of us sitting on top of the pile, in temperatures of over thirty degrees. Now to our final dismay, the gates to the stadium were locked tight, no one was anywhere to be seen and it was already 3.30 pm.

We sat another hour trying to shelter from the blazing sun before a car appeared with the two German team members who now tried to organise things for us. Then the Pastor came, finally our team leader arrived with his interpreter. We discovered the problem. The team leader had not believed that we would arrive that day, so had asked the Pastor to make alternative arrangements to bring in another sound system and for someone else to preach that night. No proper accommodation had been arranged, and that is why no one had been at the airport to meet us.

I preached a message on three reasons why God sent Jesus. Of the 3000 who were there, almost everyone came forward for salvation and the crush to receive healing was so tremendous, Rick once again feared there was no way to save the precious sound equipment from the stampede. It was the same story in every new town we went to, we had to train up afresh the few existing believers who never before had had to handle such crowds.

The Pastor was very pleased that night. No evangelist had ever come to the town before and already he was pleading with us to stay with our music group and evangelise with him all the villages and settlements where the Gospel had never been preached between here and Komsomolsk.

Saturday dawned. Looking back through our records we found it was the first restful morning we had had since Komsomolsk, exactly fifteen days before. We really relished it.

At midday about eighteen people gathered for prayer. Anxious that they were looking to me rather than to Jesus for help, I spoke to them first. "If God heals you," I said, "if He works a miracle in your life, you have a responsibility towards God. He wants you to have a relationship with Him. If you see a miracle happen and you don't love God afterwards, you will be accountable to Him. If God heals you, you owe God something, not me! God only wants one thing, He wants you to love Him. And to demonstrate that you love Him - OBEY HIM!"

The interesting thing was that in that group were two of the most outstanding miracles from last night, and it was only now that we were to learn how truly great those miracles were. The first to be healed yesterday was a middle-aged woman. She had fallen on a metal spike four days before, necessitating twenty-one stitches in her right leg. Her agonising pain suddenly went and she had made a big demonstration for the crowd to see how complete her deliverance was as she threw away her crutches and began to joyfully walk up and down. Her friends with her in the room today told us how, after the accident, she could neither sit nor stand nor walk, nor lie down, she was in such distress. Yet now she had walked to the apartment and up all those flights of stairs without pain and without assistance!

The other was a little boy held in his mother's arms. Apparently he had weak legs, but when we prayed in Jesus' Name yesterday, he put his feet down, then began to hop. Today his mother described in detail what the problem had been. He had had a deformity from birth so that he could only walk on the balls of his feet and couldn't bend his knees. His mother stood up to show us how, before, he could only swing his legs from his hips like a bear. Yet to come here he had walked up the stairs as smartly as any soldier.

Every one of the eighteen people in the room wanted prayer, and every one received their healing from the Lord. It was another wonderful experience. In the evening I had an impassioned message for the crowd, and spoke out of a deep commitment to the Lord. I said, "I won't leave you. I'll come again and again until together we break the power of Satan and until the Power of God is seen from one side of Russia to the other. How many thousands and millions of innocent men and women have died in this land ? It's stained red with blood and the blood of every innocent man, woman and child has cried out to God and God has heard every cry. The God of Heaven loves this people and this land. He wants to bless you, heal you and set you free from sin. That's why God sent Jesus. God wants to take this town and demonstrate His love.''

Because of the problem with the PA equipment yesterday a big ring was formed around the system to protect it tonight. Somehow I found myself inside this ring. I experienced some difficulty in praying for the sick at first until I realised that inadvertently I had become the centre of a bit of a circus. But as soon as we left the ring and allowed the usual inevitable crush to form around us, the healings began to flow again really quickly in the relative privacy, responding to whichever need seemed to press itself most forcefully.

On the Sunday morning it had been arranged that the whole team would visit one of the local prisons for a full service. It is always exciting for me to minister in these places because of the ten months I spent in a communist prison in Czechoslovakia.

Going through the doors, into the gloomy, despairing atmosphere brings back memories, although no longer is there the sheer terror which I experienced all those years ago. Instead it is almost exhilarating because I am free, not only to go in, but also to get out afterwards!

Our men set up the sound system and the music instruments and the praise and worship team led the first part. They sang, then between the songs, testified of what Christ had done in their lives. This always brings blessing as those who listen to these fresh young people realise how real Christ is to them. Then I spoke. Sharing something of my own experience in prison always gets the prisoners interested. When I then tell them that I know how to break the chains and get free from prison, the prisoners either pull their chairs closer, or eagerly strain forward in the crowd. I watch the prison guards get a little apprehensive as I mention getting out. However today it is Christ who is going to set them free, not me, and they gladly accept the word of the Lord. My joy is to see everyone signify their desire to accept Christ - which they did! Afterwards I learned that in the prison is a regular Bible class and some of the prisoners have already found salvation; they will encourage the new believers to become grounded in the faith.

The Pastor told us that a year ago the church had had a prophecy that they would see 4000 people saved and added to the church in one weekend. They had thought that this was impossible, no hall in town could seat anywhere near this number. Then they realised that the only place large enough was the football stadium, but how could they take it? When they heard that we were coming there for the Crusade, they were excited. But only when they finally saw over 6500 accept Christ in the three days did they realise that God had fulfilled His promise and even given more. They wanted us to stay and evangelise the whole area. Not this time, but by God's grace we will be back to fulfil everything in His prophecy to us. Only a few months later as Misha began his detailed organisation for next year, 1995, Sovietskaya was amongst the first to re-confirm their invitation to us to come back and we will go.

Once again the Crusade has ended and we are again tired but exhilarated by all that God has done. But how do we get out of the town? The airport is small, and there is only one scheduled flight leaving per day and only to Khabarovsk. In faith, and to overcome the problems in getting to Neryungri, I had booked seats on the 11.00 am flight from Khabarovsk to Neryungri when I was last in Khabarovsk. It would surely be possible to get this flight, because when I had checked, the airport records had shown that there was an early morning flight from Sovietskaya Gavan landing at Khabarovsk at 9.00 am. It was only on arriving in Sovietskaya itself that I found, not surprisingly I suppose, that this flight did not exist! So the airport director had offered to arrange for the same chartered AN 28 which had brought us here to return and collect us at 8.00 am on the Monday.

Arriving at the airport early on the Monday morning with the group, there was no sign of our charter plane. Once again the Zavtra spirit was at work. Leaving the group to enjoy the morning sun outside, Svetlana and I went in to make enquiries. The airport manager was busy, so in urgent desperation we wandered without hindrance into the operations room. No one there knew of any incoming aircraft. Urgently they checked both radar and radio, but there was nothing on the screen or any report of any aircraft coming. At my insistence the staff finally got through to the small airport at Khabarovsk by radio and we discovered to our amazement that the AN 28 was still on the ground with no flight plan to take off! Even if it took off immediately it would take ninety minutes to arrive, ninety minutes to return, plus the time for us to load. It would be far too late for us to make the connection with the scheduled flight leaving at 11.00 am for Neryungri. We would lose our tickets and the money we had paid, but more importantly, we would not make it to the next Crusade. Once again the Zavtra spirit had tried to defeat us. But, Hallelujah, I know Jesus defeated both Satan and the Zavtra spirit 2000 years ago and I am going to live, not in defeat, but in victory. In Jesus' Name I will win this battle; the devil just gets me more determined than ever!

Once more I went back to the group enjoying their freedom in the warm sunshine outside and asked them to pray desperately for another miracle, another really big miracle this time. Out here in Siberia nothing seems to go according to plan. The airport staff don't care if you fly or not, they have no desire to help or make money for the State-owned monopoly, or even do a real day's work. Usually they say no just to avoid having to work at anything. The morale is so appallingly low.

Going back slowly towards the building my eyes took in the scene before me, a woman trying to wash and clean the broken steps leading up to the door. In her hands she held a broom which she had obviously made herself earlier that morning, because the small branches which she had tied clumsily together still had the green leaves on them, not even dried out. Her task was made more difficult because she had not changed the water in her bucket and it was a muddy brown in colour.

Stepping through the door, I can still see in my mind's eye the small dark lobby, the inner door which was stiff to open, leading to the inner room which had a few simple seats and a counter where supposedly one could check-in. Next to it was the small box-like room with a glass front panel where on better days hopeful travellers could buy tickets. At the moment, apparently there were no staff on duty so the dirty curtain which hid the interior was drawn shut, not in defiance but rather in despair. After all there would be no airplanes so why work!

Climbing the stairs to the manager's office a sense of urgency once again took hold of me. His meeting was not over but I just went in and began to ask him what had gone wrong with his arrangement for the charter aircraft. His explanation would not solve the problem, I did not have time to waste on words, just action, and fast. I am rather impatient at the best of times, now more than ever. "I need an aircraft now, I want it ready to take off in ten minutes or we miss the connection at Khabarovsk." Of course I had personally never succeeded before in getting airplanes chartered with less than a day's notice, now I needed it to be in the air and flying in less than twenty-four minutes! Talk of miracles, this would be the biggest yet if I was successful. For once he reacted quickly, there were no normal aircraft at all within hundreds of miles, only his emergency helicopter which we had seen on the ground when we landed. But his pilots were in the room with us and yes, if we paid now, in roubles, we could have it immediately. It was already 8.00 am, so I sent one of the other girls from the music team who had come with us, Asya, to tell everyone to move quickly. If we took more than thirty minutes now we would definitely miss our connection.

With help from the church members who had driven us up in their cars and were still so kindly waiting, all the equipment was moved to the check-in and weighed. By the time I had signed the contract and found the necessary money, part in roubles and part in dollars the cars were already on their way across the tarmac. Quickly we loaded everything as the pilots dragged the big hose pipe across to re-fuel the helicopter for the flight. The big 26 seat military flying machine was filthy. The crew loaded what appeared to be smelly, dripping sacks of fish. They were obviously going to do some trade on arrival. The smell and the dirt added to the inevitable noise, but it was just twenty-four minutes after I had made the request that the big jet motors burst into raucous life. 8.45 am and the awkward brute clumsily dragged itself reluctantly along the tarmac and lazily lifted into the air. Only God knows how I managed it, but I had taken the devil head-on and beaten him and his Zavtra spirit by the authority and power I have in Jesus' Name! If only every born again, Spirit filled believer knew what power and authority we have over Satan.

The flight to the airport at Khabarovsk took us 1 hour 45 minutes in the rather slow helicopter. It was an awesome experience. The cloud base was quite low, below 3000 feet, and the hills very high. The pilot needed to keep visual contact with the ground, so because the mountain peaks were much higher than the clouds, he flew between the tops of the mountains, twisting and turning the helicopter, in order to keep below the cloud level at times only feet above him. Several times the rugged rock face of the hills on both sides of us seemed only feet away from the urgently spinning rotor blades by which we were perilously suspended. If the blades which held the heavily loaded machine in the air just brushed one of those rocks which loomed out of the mist and cloud - so close that it seemed that we could reach out and touch them - we would crash hundreds of feet into the valley. Rescue was out of the question because this was the only rescue helicopter and we were flying in it!

As always God was in control and after a long hour and three quarters the buildings of a large town at last came into view and we left the mountains behind us. It was 10.30 by our watches when we landed the helicopter at the same small airport which we had left four days before. Only minutes to unload, transport everything to the bigger airport and check-in.

We made it, getting the tickets and finding transport to move everything the few hundred yards separating the two airfields. We caught the flight with moments to spare, but the whole thing was a miracle which only God could have performed.

Chapter 17

NERYUNGRI - THE VALLEY OF DEATH

The scheduled flight from Khabarovsk to Neryungri was in a YAK 40, a small 38 seat jet. The only problem with this aircraft was that it had no cargo bay. You enter by a door with its own drop down steps, leading directly into the rear of the plane. Unfortunately the door into the jet cannot be opened very wide because the toilet is situated immediately behind it, protruding into the passageway. Luggage can only be stowed in two metal racks on the right hand side behind the toilet, room enough for a few bags, yes, but not for all the two tons of music equipment and sound system, as well as our own odd assortment of luggage. It was the loudspeakers which posed us the biggest problem in these YAK 40's, as it was almost impossible to get them past the toilet door! On this flight there were also twenty-six other passengers who had already boarded and whose baggage seemed to completely fill the limited luggage space before we could start to load ours. We had been rather late in boarding due to the intransigence of the woman at the check-in.

Although half of us had the more expensive west or 'Intourist' tickets, we preferred, if we could, to check-in together at the Russian side. This meant that the men could share the heavy task of moving the equipment, also that the excess baggage weight of nearly two tons could be charged against the cheaper price of Russian rather than Western tickets, literally saving hundreds of dollars on each of the many flights.

The woman at the desk who had at first accepted us all without question, suddenly changed her mind because she had heard one of us speaking English! Now half of us had to dash several hundred yards away into the separate building reserved for Intourist, but worse, we first had to pull out half of the equipment already checked and accepted for the flight and re-weigh it to subtract from the excess baggage charge, drag it up the road, then commence the check-in all over again!

As we were the last to board, we tried desperately to fit our impedimenta into the available space but without avail. By now the crew were urging us to hurry, but what could we do? Passing as much as possible inside we began to load it into the passenger space. Starting at the front, I blocked off the only exit from the pilot's cockpit, put bags and amplifiers in front of startled passengers' legs, filled the seats which our own staff needed with bags, then put the remainder right down the centre gangway. Finally we got it all in, but how! Remember that we had a total of about forty pieces of equipment and luggage with us and the aircraft was only small! No normal western airline would have allowed the central gangway and the exits to be blocked as we had done, also what about the question of the total weight on the aircraft? But if you want to ask, what about the rest of the things which we saw on this same flight, dogs and hamsters and every other conceivable and inconceivable thing.

Svetlana and I had already flown this route before on our way up to Aldan, so the arrival at Neryungri was no real surprise to us. The military came on board checking all the visas as before because not only was Aldan a closed city, but this was also. However to our relief this time everything was in order - Svetlana and I had collected the visa for the whole group from the Pastor on our previous visit.

Getting off the plane we had to load everything on to the airport bus as usual. Then the bus set off on a twenty minute drive out of the airport itself, past the police barriers which controlled this closed area, round some rough roads, through the forest and past the small, but picturesque log cabins which, with other industrial buildings, dotted the mountainous terrain. Finally we saw the evidence of a small town, before finally arriving at the terminal building. This is the only place I know where the airport is miles away from its own terminal and check-in.

Some of the Ukrainians from our ground team were here waiting for us, so they soon helped us to transfer everything onto the bus which would take us to the main town where the rest of the team were waiting to welcome us. Pastor Gorbachev and his team who had come down from Aldan to help with the Crusade soon helped us to get to the various apartments where we would stay for the next three days. It was good to be back with friends.

What a relief to be on schedule and arrive the day before the Crusade, to be able to relax and prepare for the meeting! The schedule said, "Monday, travel", and we had not only travelled but actually arrived on the same day we set out!

Next night the Crusade began in a sports hall where a big crowd gathered and many received Christ. I preached on Romans 10, " 'If you will confess with your mouth that Jesus is Lord and believe in your heart that God raised him from the dead you will be saved.' How can you be saved if you have not believed, and how can you believe if you have not heard? We have come so that you may know this Jesus - how much He loves us, how much He cares."

Here again special healings took place. The Pastor's daughter was healed of an abdominal hernia. It went down bit by bit. The mother, who was checking with her hand as we prayed, suddenly became very excited and lifted up the little girl's dress to look. The hernia had completely gone. Two months after our Crusade an article by a somewhat sceptical author appeared in one of the English Christian newspapers. He had called his contacts in Siberia in some of the cities where we had been and heard everywhere the healings were confirmed. A certain Iida he spoke to in Neryungri told him of a woman healed of 'a problem with the woman's part of the body'. Her healing had continued. Also there was a deaf girl Iida knew of who could now hear and a woman who had previously been unable to walk unaided but could now walk by herself. We praise God for this independent witness of the demonstration of His power.

Svetlana and I stayed in the same apartment we had stayed in before on our way to Aldan about a month previously. Our hostess was, as I said, a refugee from the villages destroyed as a result of the accident at the Chernobyl nuclear reactor and resulting explosion in 1986. This had resulted in the governments of Belarus and the Ukraine evacuating many thousands, so she and her husband with their twelve year old son, had been moved here, some 6,000 miles from their home. Unfortunately her husband had since left her, but she had just recently found Christ. Her home was special and different, bigger, better equipped and more modern. She was a wonderful hostess preparing a beautiful meal for us each evening and, although she had to leave early for work each day, she prepared food in advance for Svetlana to heat up for us at lunch time. Because of the size of this apartment and as she was out all day, we were able to get some of the other members of the team to join us in order to spend time in prayer.

It was on the third day, Wednesday, when something really demonic happened. The central team had joined me for prayer, after which some church members brought a woman, Tanya, for me to cast out an evil spirit. She had made a decision to receive Christ at the same time as our hostess; they were friends. But when the church members had prayed for them both to receive the Holy Spirit, only our hostess had received. This other woman told me that she had gone out into the woods alone, and there received 'a spirit'.

I remembered our Pastor friend from Blagoveshchensk had told us that this town was situated in what they called the 'Valley of Death'. That is actually the meaning of its name. The story is that although the town was relatively new, this place had been known for centuries as the place where men and animals would come to die. There was obviously a strong spirit controlling this area. Tanya had clearly become possessed by an evil spirit. She could certainly speak in another language as if 'speaking in tongues' when the demon manifested itself and it also recognised and spoke English. When we began to pray we were joined by Pastor Gorbachev and the senior members of his ground team, as well as our intercessors and the local Pastor.

This spirit had a very powerful control over the woman. When I spoke to it commanding that it should go in the Name of Jesus, Tanya said that she was married to Satan. We discovered that her grandmother and aunt were involved in witchcraft and that even her fourteen year old daughter wanted to be a witch.

The spirit spoke to me in English, saying, "I know who you are," but when the Pastor began to pray, it asked who he was. Suddenly it took control of the woman again and began to make her dance, then go into a whirling ritual as if trying to cast spells on us. Again I commanded that it should leave, this time saying that if it refused, I would cast it into the fires of hell. Suddenly it screamed out in response, "Anything but that, anything but that, don't send me there!" Tanya then said, "The spirit will go if you will only bring my daughter here." The devil's designs on the young girl were horrendously obvious and we refused. We took authority again in Jesus' Name, commanding it to come out, which finally it did, but only after a hard battle which continued after the service that night and into the early hours of the following morning.

The greatest difficulty we had was in convincing the local church members that Tanya was free. Sometimes we become so impressed by the current teachings about demons that fear is introduced and we are almost tempted to depart from our simple faith in Christ. In Him we are new creations, the old has passed away - 2 Corinthians 5:17. This over-emphasis on demons was at times a stumbling block in a number of the churches we visited and a source of fear and bondage to new believers.

This was only one of many very strong evil spirits which we met while in these remote parts of Siberia. The communists had tried to keep all mention of God from the land, by banning Bibles, faith in Christ, imprisoning and killing many believers. The result was that they had left the land wide open for many evil spirits to come. Witchcraft and the occult have thrived here along with demons and false religions.

Despite this attempt by the devil to disrupt and distract me, the service that night was again very powerful, many came forward for salvation, then after for healing. Almost before I had finished praying the opening prayer, a middle-aged woman in a purple outfit detached herself from the crowds and came walking towards me in tears, beautifully erect, carrying her crutches in her hand. She had been instantly set free! As we prayed individually a little girl who had come to us deaf and dumb found she could say "Mama, Papa, Anya" and spoke into the microphone for the camera as Phil recorded this miracle. The most moving of all was a young woman, only eighteen or nineteen, who came to me with her mother. She had cancer lumps in both breasts and as I placed my hands on hers I felt her hot tears falling. Because of this I prayed most persistently. Then hope began to show in her face. "The lumps are getting smaller," she said. "Now they are gone, but I still feel as if something's there." I would not give up praying. Finally she said, "Everything's gone. I'm well!"

The following morning, Thursday, on the way to the airport the Pastor took us to the local hospital to pray. Going up to one of the wards the first patient was a young man, a backslider. Badly beaten up by the Mafia, he had a clot on the brain; God delivered him. The next was a middle-aged man, about six foot six inches tall, with a broken back only able to walk painfully with crutches. Instantly the power of God healed him so that all pain went and he could walk unaided. Watching was a young man with a cracked vertebra. When I offered to pray there was not even a flicker of faith in his eyes. Yet he instantly stood up in amazement, healed! The nurses, including the Matron, who were looking on, were so thrilled that they now asked me to pray for a man in another ward. They said that he had a demon, and he was obviously very disturbed when I went in.

Lying on a special bed he was in a bad way. He said that he had very severe head pain but in addition his legs, hip and ribs were broken and his whole body was racked with pain which was driving him out of his mind. Starting with his head I asked him, "If God will heal your head, will you believe in Him?" He replied, "Yes." When I touched him all the pain went. I discovered that he was a murderer and had killed many people, but here he was, pleading with me to heal his legs which were hurting so much. So I asked him another question, "If God heals your broken legs will you stop killing people?" Again he replied, "Yes!" At that moment the power of God literally swept through his body and he was healed, hallelujah!

By now the nurses were laughing, but tears ran down their cheeks. They had witnessed an amazing demonstration of the power of God to bless even a man so evil as this murderer, whom I learned was out of one of the prisons. It was difficult to leave this hospital, they all demanded attention when they saw the many miracles. But time was short and we needed to catch the flight which we had booked. What a wonderful way to leave town with such a positive demonstration of the anointing of the Holy Spirit resting on us, right to the end. So it was with this evidence of God's power that we resumed our journey up to the airport building for our flight on to the next Crusade in Magadan, the most notorious town in the whole of Siberia.

Chapter 18

MAGADAN - THE DEATH CAMP

For once we had no problem in leaving the town after our visit. From Neryungri we had already got air tickets booked for the first leg of our 1200 mile journey to Magadan via Yakutsk.

While waiting for the flight I took some of the team including Phil White, our cameraman, out to the back of the airport building to see the scene of an earlier miracle. This was the place where God had provided the helicopter to take Svetlana and me down to Blagoveshchensk over a month previously. For the record it was good both to film the actual place where it happened and show the others the actual aircraft 'junk yard'.

The flight to Yakutsk was routine. Flying north east was an experience, especially as we would fly over the town of Aldan where I had held one of the earlier Crusades on this programme. I had also been through Yakutsk once previously on this Siberian Adventure. On the way from Susuman to Chita I had rescued the Czech team from Yakutsk, but it was still very interesting to view from the air the hills and forests leading to this region. The typical Siberian landscape is scarred by man-made clearings and some apparent gold mine workings, which then gave way to the flatter area as we approached the river on which Yakutsk is situated. The town itself is not attractive, but the surrounding scenery, especially on the river, is. Despite the apparent remoteness of Yakutsk, not far from the Arctic Circle, it is an important centre. The big river carries much of the commercial trade for the region, but only in the short summer season. In winter it becomes very cold, temperatures even go below minus 50 degrees centigrade, and the river freezes over. The region has its own unique weather pattern, I am told, so that it is reputedly colder here in Yakutsk than anywhere on earth, even than the North Pole.

Landing at the airport, I hurried into the terminal ahead of the others to enquire about the possibility of a connection on to Magadan. You see in Siberia they have a problem which caused us the greatest difficulty in travelling between the Crusade towns and cities. Airports like Neryungri which we had just left, could reserve us tickets for the first leg of the journey such as we had just taken into Yakutsk, but could not tell us what flights there would be out of the airport at which we would arrive - in this case Yakutsk - let alone book them for us. Their computers could only deal with their own flight departures and were not connected into any central system. I don't think that there is such a system anyway. But in order to link in to any such computerised reservation programme, if there was one, they would need a direct telephone line. That, as we had discovered, there definitely is not. That was the real problem.

Landing at the airport I took one of the Ukrainians from our team as interpreter and went into the terminal to ask about flights to Magadan. I suppose by now I should have realised the futility of even asking. Today was Thursday, August 11th, the next flight into Magadan was not until Saturday 13th, but in any case there was not a single ticket available for about two or three weeks. So to get tickets for a group of eleven persons was a joke. But the Crusade in Magadan was to start tomorrow evening, Friday 12th. God has told me to go, and I'm on my way, but how? No wonder, when I asked the Lord how on earth I would be able to win Siberia, the answer had been so positive - by miracles, signs and wonders! In all my life I have never witnessed as many miracles as we were experiencing here.

However here I was, facing the inevitable, with the time change we had lost another couple of hours so it was after 5.00 pm, and of course the Aeroflot offices were now closed until 8.00 am the next day. Well, thank God that we could still pray, because there was nothing else we could do. Except find somewhere to park all the equipment at the airport ready for an early start next day, and find somewhere for the whole weary group to spend another night. Of course, although they were not complaining yet, there were some members of the team who needed food, since we had not eaten since breakfast.

I am beginning to think that as the Evangelist, someone ought to relieve me of all this responsibility. Maybe one day God will answer my repeated cry of "Help!" and send me a capable, qualified organiser. He needs to be able to speak fluent Russian, understand all the cultural problems in Siberia, how to work non-existent telephones, have experience as a travel agent, the ability to call down dollars from Heaven daily, work without food and sleep for days on end, understand the way Russians think, and others don't think, have the faith of Abraham, the leadership qualities of Moses, the determination and love of God that David had, be able to walk on water, move mountains. And all that, just to get through yesterday!

As one of my personal intercessors said, "No one else would be fool enough to try, so God called you to do it, and He has spent a lifetime training you."

Yet God is still in the business of answering prayers, one at a time. So we found somewhere to park the equipment, and also an 'airport hotel' across the road. Doss-house maybe, but at least it had beds to go with the mosquitoes and cockroaches. Food? Well personally I've forgotten that bit and I've lost a lot of weight, but I know God did answer that too!

Morning staggered round to dawning as usual next day and I was up early enough to try to stumble into the Aeroflot offices before the staff were sufficiently awake to remember such words as "Niet", and "Zavtra". What are the Russian words for, "Yes, sir" and "Pleased to help you" or, "We have airplanes, would you like to charter one now, sir?" Sadly this was no vision, it was only a daydream!

The airport directors were not available when we enquired in the offices. A surprisingly helpful woman informed us politely that we should wait patiently as it would take two full days to organise a charter flight. But the Crusade begins tonight! The main problem now was that there was no one else except this woman in the office. She told us that the directors were all outside on the runway supervising the departure of the President of the Yakut Autonomous Republic who was flying to London.

To emphasise the problems which we now faced here in Yakutsk, I remembered the desperate appeal for help from our Czech group who themselves had been stranded here until I had rescued them some weeks earlier. As if to discourage me more, a group of twenty Russians came in at that moment. They had been stranded for the past two weeks with no possibility of either scheduled or charter flight out. It seemed to demonstrate you could only get into Yakutsk, not out!

Not only were my own special intercessors praying earnestly into the situation, but I was also sitting on a hard chair refusing to leave the office, asking God for a solution. One can have positive faith for a situation, but in order to be specific in both my request to God and have the faith to fulfil it, I needed to know what I wanted. At the moment I wanted the airport director to get back so that I could discuss my request for a charter flight with him, because as yet I had not even submitted an official request to Aeroflot, for them to either accept or reject. My only contact was with this insignificant looking woman; she, not the directors, had refused my request. Who was she?

Now a young man came urgently and purposefully into the room. He was talking to the woman behind the desk in Russian so I took no special notice of him, thinking that this was just one more stranded passenger. Svetlana may have overheard the private conversation, but she did not translate it.

Suddenly Svetlana did begin to translate; the woman was now speaking, "Maybe this young man can help you." "Well," I demanded directly, "I need to charter an aircraft to fly into Magadan at once, to leave within an hour." His reply was so simple, "The President is flying into London right now, I can charter you his own private jet, a YAK 40, you can indeed be in the air within an hour!"

What an answer! No forty-eight hour delay, no problems - and what an airplane for us - the Presidential jet! I obviously did not hesitate for longer than it took to ask the price, which was reasonable. I did not question what right he had to give us the President's own airplane. My Bible says, "My God will supply!" I had not thought to ask God for a luxurious airplane, I just asked Him to solve the problem and get us into Magadan. He had called me to go, and He must provide. But the President's luxury jet, wow! Now I feel like a King's son!

Our team were all waiting, including the cameraman, Phil, whom I had sent earlier that morning into town to change dollars into roubles because I so knew that we would have the plane today, and it had to be paid for with roubles. They would not accept dollars for payment on any of these charters.

Soon everything was loaded, and we relaxed in the luxury of the comfortable swivel chairs with tables, thick carpet, and the pleasant decor, vastly different to a normal Russian aircraft, especially some of the cargo planes and military helicopters which we had previously chartered. But God does like to surprise us and bless us, just to show how much He loves and cares. The Ukrainians, especially the girls, Elena, Asya, and Gallya in the praise and worship team were really excited by it all. They had never seen anything like this before!

The flight time in this swift airplane was only two and a quarter hours, but again we lost a further two hours because we were travelling almost due east, across two time zones, landing at the Magadan airport just before 5.00 pm local time. I sensed that the devil was very determinedly attacking us; the meeting tonight should be in the football stadium but as we stepped onto the tarmac, the rain fell in torrents from black, threatening clouds. This surely is one of the worst places on earth, the nearest to a living hell, as we would soon be reminded.

Oleg whom we had met en route to Susuman, was waiting to welcome us with men and vehicles to hasten us into the town, first to the hotel, then quickly to the stadium. Because of the weather this first meeting had been hastily re-located in a sports hall right at the side of the stadium. The enemy was trying desperately to stop the Crusade and this was the first time that a meeting had been moved because of the weather. Normally we would just take authority over the weather in Jesus' Name, but we had arrived too late to do this effectively tonight. Ultimately even for us tiredness could and did weaken our spiritual effectiveness. Tomorrow would be a different story, God would miraculously change the weather. But now, a small group, mainly of believers from the local supporting church, gathered together with our own ground team in the hastily re-organised meeting.

Yes, God was there and we did see some few decisions, and there were some outstanding miracles of healing. An old man, deaf in his left ear could hear and the paralysis in his arm and leg went completely. A middle-aged woman was next in the line, seriously ill with a cancerous lump in her left breast and pain from a broken spine. As I laid my hands on her in the Name of Jesus, she was set free from all pain and the lump disappeared from her breast! A man who was dumb began to speak, a young woman born with serious eye defects was instantly healed. Many others were healed of kidney problems, blindness and arthritic pains. Jesus is still in business to destroy the works of the devil - even in Magadan!

The next morning we met the ground team for intercession. There were some wonderful people in this team, different in character from the other teams we had worked with. They had flown direct from England into Magadan and had not had any experience of the other areas, just this one here. They were a very faithful team and had some strong intercessors with them. These were needed desperately in this town which historically had a terrible experience of suffering and death.

The Crusade that Saturday night was in the stadium and the sun shone warmly despite the approaching winter. You see God works many miracles and in the hall the previous night I had publicly taken authority over the weather, which I had done many times throughout these Crusades. If we are going to take Siberia for Jesus, we must demonstrate the power and authority which we have in His Name.

A crowd had gathered, but still smaller than we had expected. It seems as if there is something here which needs breaking. The devil is determined, but so am I and well over half of those present come forward to respond to the Gospel. But this is still not the breakthrough which we had prayed for. Ever since we had been in Siberia, those of us in the central team had been praying and looking for the moment when a significant breakthrough would occur. Rick, with Phil and Gary, had spent much time in prayer during the day on the mountain overlooking the town, believing that Magadan was indeed the place where God would pour out His power. I believe that I do know what will happen, but not when, because the times are in God's hands. This in itself is awakening the challenge within me to return next year, 'in the power of the Spirit'. There have been some remarkable confirmations since from many unexpected sources of the prophetic vision God revealed to me about Magadan.

Significantly I saw many miracles of healing that night, outstanding for the relatively small number present, and many of them are recorded on video film. One of the first was an older woman who had broken her back when she was only three years old and suffered all her life. By the authority which I have in Jesus' Name, I now set her instantly free. She was so excited it was difficult for her to contain her joy. Another old woman who was able to walk only with the aid of a crutch and who had a damaged spine and arthritis in her knees was so dramatically healed that she did an impromptu 'Cossack' dance in front of the crowd! Many other healings followed, too many to mention, and that was just the ones for whom I prayed. The other members of the ground team also saw miracles amongst the sick they prayed for.

After supper at the Pastor's apartment, he took us down to the bay where we could see the old harbour area. Standing on the beach where so much of the horror of this town had begun we tried to visualise the scene.

Originally, more than a hundred years ago, some Americans had come here to this place and had decided that the climate and general conditions were so severe that no human could possibly survive them. It was obviously with this in mind that Stalin had created the place as a death camp. To reach Magadan the prisoners had first been carried across Russia and Siberia for thousands of miles by train, on the Trans Siberian Railway. This would have taken up to three weeks, but not in luxury; tightly packed into cattle trucks, when they arrived at the end of the railway line at Vladivostok it was almost impossible to tell the difference between the living and the dead. If during the journey, they died from the inhumane conditions, they were nonetheless crammed together so tightly that they still remained upright. Only when the doors were opened and they were let out did the guards know which ones were still alive. Then the prisoners were put on ships and brought up the coast to the awful death which still remained before them at Magadan.

Most of the year the harbour was frozen over because of the extremely low temperatures, yet still the prison ships came. Walking barefoot the prisoners were then forced to cross the ice and snow leading on to the beach and up to the rough buildings. No wonder that if any of the prisoners from other parts of Russia were told that they were condemned to go to Magadan they rebelled in horror, pleading with their captors not to send them there. Even death itself was better than the horror of Magadan, hell on earth.

Now we had come here to set the captives free from death and hell, by the power and authority of the Name of Jesus.

With memories of my own imprisonment in mind, I asked the Pastor what kind of work the prisoners had done. His reply was stark and cold, "There was no work here, they only came here to die." When the first human consignments had arrived there were no buildings, so they had to erect their own crude shelter from the appallingly cold weather, then gradually build more substantial houses. There were no walls or barriers round Magadan to stop prisoners escaping, since there was absolutely nowhere to go. Outside of the small town itself the whole region is inhospitable. In winter, just a barren expanse of snow and ice, even in the brief summer, there was no food or shelter outside the settlement. How could you survive? If you go to the north you are approaching the

Arctic Circle, to the east, only the cruel sea, to the west, many hundreds of miles without any form of habitation, to the south, the same. Truly this was hell with no way of escaping. No wonder Alexander Solzhenitsyn, the famous Russian author, who himself was incarcerated here for a time describes such horror in his book, *Gulag Archipelago*.

Pastor Nikolai described how that if any prisoner did escape, no one attempted to stop him, he would simply be one more to die. If any one returned and succeeded in getting back in without being detected, he would not be punished. But if the returning escapee was seen, they would let him return, letting him think he was safe, then would shoot him in the back. This way it appeared as if it was only escaping prisoners who were shot.

Showing us the roads, which now were covered with rough tarmac, he told us how that under the communist regime, prisoners were compelled to make the roads from earth and stones. Each prisoner was allocated a section of the road for which he had responsibility and had to keep it smooth and free from bumps or holes. This was extremely difficult because of the extreme weather conditions and lack of materials. If an officer rode over any section and found a small irregularity, the prisoner responsible was summoned, forced to dig a hole in this section where the flaw was, then he was shot and buried in the hole he had dug. His section was then allocated to another prisoner. This meant that every road in the town was literally laid on the bones of the prisoners who had died.

Sunday morning came and it was a wonderful opportunity for me to speak and encourage the local church, which had about three hundred members. I said:

> I come to Siberia, with a burning vision of the Power of
> God. When God speaks He speaks with power and

authority. Today I want to speak by prophecy and by vision of what God wants to accomplish - and God will accomplish what He says. He cannot fail. I want you to burn with the fire and passion of God.

We have seen so many great miracles in Siberia, but it's only the beginning of what God wants to do. These are the last days immediately before the return of Christ and God's going to do something that will startle the whole world. God is about to release power and do miracles and wonders that have never been recorded in the history of the Bible - but they are recorded in the prophecy of the Bible for the future!

For one year I have been burning with the vision of what God will do here. There are prophecies from many different parts of Russia about what God will do in this nation in these days. God showed me the revival must begin here in the east and these prophecies say the same. The Far East, Magadan, Sovietskaya Gavan, is where God is going to begin.

In Deuteronomy 4 it's not a prophet but it's actually God speaking. In verse 32 He speaks of an event so amazing it's never been recorded in the history of the world. In verse 33 and 34 God is speaking to us today - what He did for Israel, He's going to do for us - He's going to take a nation from within a nation and the eyes of the whole world will look to see the miracles God will do. God is about to do this today!

In Joel 2:23 God says, "Be glad ... for He will pour out the former and the latter rain." In verse 28 He says, "I will pour out My Spirit on all flesh, and in verses 30-31, He says "I will show wonders in the Heaven and on the earth

... before the great and terrible day of the Lord.''

The first part of this prophecy was fulfilled on the first day of Pentecost when the Church was born in the fire of the Holy Spirit. This was the former rain but there will be a second and greater outpouring of Pentecost immediately before the return of the Lord - the latter rain. Then Christ will come in a cloud of Glory to a Church that has seen the revelation of the Glory of Jesus Christ. Yes, He will come to a world that rejects Him, but that also knows and recognises Him through the signs and wonders.

God is waiting to find a people on whom He can pour out His Spirit. God wants to lift up the Name of Jesus on the face of the whole earth. But the place God has chosen for the greatest outpouring is here. Nowhere has so denied the power of God. This is the place where so many millions were slaughtered. No other nation has seen such slaughter. Your entire society was built on the denial of God and the devil has had more power here than anywhere else in the world. But his power is broken and God has chosen THIS place to demonstrate HIS Power.

I want to show you how to bring down the Power of God. The reason I first went to Jerusalem thirty years ago was because I was seeking THIS Pentecost. It didn't come, but fire entered MY soul, hunger was born in ME. Pentecost HAD begun.

You can experience it. I want to show you how. We could take Magadan in a day! No one can say ''no''. I'm not going to rest till the Fire rests on YOU and YOU and YOU!

In Numbers 14:11 God spoke to Moses, "How long will these people provoke Me and refuse to believe in Me despite all the signs and wonders I have performed among them?" - This is the rebuke to the whole nation of Russia. God says He will work wonders, right in front of your eyes, in front of the whole nation, then He will give the challenge of Numbers 14:11, "How long will you refuse to believe in Me despite all that I have done?"

Who's going to work the miracles? God! Through you! And me! God has called us! Revival will not come to England till Russia's on fire! I've seen the Fire and the Power of God - my father was born in revival and worked with the greatest healing evangelist in Britain, George Jeffries. And this same George Jeffries was the one who took me in his arms and dedicated me to the Lord. He prayed the fire of God into me.

God says He's got to do miracles HERE. I want to turn the eyes of the whole world here to see what God is doing! God has given me a vision for Magadan. Read Ezekiel 37, the Valley of Dry Bones. God said to the prophet, "Go and stand where all the dead are in the Valley of Death, where the people were slain in their thousands and millions." How many children of God, how many pastors, how many leaders died here in Magadan? Go and stand over the places where those men of God died. Get filled with the Holy Ghost now - pray and praise till the Fire comes down and when it does, one of you will go out into those fields and you will prophesy and those graves will open, that valley will open up and those believers who died will come out of the ground and stand here and preach the Gospel to the whole town. Prophesy over your towns, over your fields until the dead come back and preach the Gospel. If one of those dead prisoners came back , the TV cameras of the whole world would come here!

Now look! In Numbers 14:13-16, Moses has an argument with God because the people haven't believed the miracles and God says He'll destroy the people. Moses pleads for the people, pleads for the Church. He says, "If You turn your back on Your own people, on the Church because they haven't believed You, the whole world will say that You have failed. They will not blame the Church, they will blame You Lord. The whole world will say, "It was because the Lord was not able. If You do not fulfil every promise You have given, then the eyes of the whole world will look and say, 'God has failed.' "

This is the assurance that God will pour out His Spirit and work these miracles, because, God, if You don't do what You promised, the world will say that YOU have failed, that You could not keep Your Word.

God heard Moses and God answered Moses. He said, "I have pardoned this people according to Your Word."

God, YOU must fulfil every vision and every prophecy.

Jesus is coming and God is going to fulfil everything now! Ezekiel 12:21-28 says, "Now is the day for the fulfilment of EVERY vision, every prophecy, every Word I have spoken." NOW! NOW! NOW! God cannot fail.

But what does it need? - Men and women to stand before God to claim the promise, call down the Power and go out and do the Work of God.

How? In Hebrews and James you'll find the answer. Hebrews 11:8 tells us Abraham was a man of faith. There are two ways God will never fail to fulfil the vision, there are two things God requires. First, faith to believe God, to go out and do it. Faith isn't sitting in your seat, get out and do it! *(The whole Church stood up.)*

Second, get to know God. What is it with Abraham? James 2 tells us he obeyed God. He did it! Are you hearing God, the voice and the power of God ? Then obey Him!

The Power comes through faith and obedience! Get up and do it! Preach the Gospel! Get up on the hills around Magadan - call on God for the Power of the Holy Spirit - then obey Him and do it!

After lunch with Pastor Nikolai and his wife we went to the stadium for the final meeting of this Crusade. News of the mighty miracles which God had done the previous night had spread throughout the town and brought a crowd of people which doubled the size of the attendance. Again a large number responded to the Gospel when I spoke and they were counselled both by me and Pastor Nikolai. Following this it was time to witness the power of God in healing and miracles. I expect the power of God and I am never disappointed because God always honours faith.

A lovely little girl was helped through the big crowd in front of me. She was on crutches because she had broken her leg two months before in a car accident. The poor girl could no longer bend her knee or put any weight on her leg, but after I took authority, the pain left. She had been so afraid of the pain that at first she had difficulty in believing. With gentle persuasion her confidence gradually returned and she began to walk unaided, then she squatted down, bending both her knees, completely healed. Next was a man also on crutches because of an accident he had had in the factory where he worked. For eighteen months after the accident the bones and muscles had not mended and as a result he was crippled. After I laid my hands on him he was immediately healed, and he walked unaided for the first time. Then the power of God began to fall upon the people so that one after the other they were delivered from arthritis, broken arms, paralysed arms and even curvature of the spine. Many others received sight and were delivered from deafness, as well as other diseases, too many of them to count, so great was God's power that night.

Many times I had told the crowds in the Crusades that along with the other members of my central team, I had only bought a one way ticket to Siberia. In fact I used to joke that, just like the prisoners who only had one way tickets, the authorities in Russia would only issue one way tickets to us.

The fact was that while we had bought return tickets from London to Moscow and Moscow to London, we had not purchased the necessary tickets to return us from Siberia to Moscow. We had expected that as in the previous year we could obtain the return to Moscow more cheaply in Chita, but this was not possible because of the problems with the airport. The other problem was that we had struggled all the way through Siberia to keep within the budget, but costs were rising almost daily. Once we had registered in a hotel at Blagoveshchensk at a certain price, only to find that next day the price had gone up by exactly 30% and we had to pay the remaining days for the whole group at the increased price. Air fares had also increased by 30% while we were in Siberia and the price of everything from food to fares varied from place to place. For example, with wages for the local population varying from $20 per month in the Ukraine up to $200 per month in the Far East of Siberia, the cost of food and everything else varied enormously. In Aldan for example, potatoes cost up to $9 per kilo (approximately £2.50 per pound), possibly ten times the price they would be elsewhere. Airfares cost almost three times as much to fly in and out of Magadan as from airports also in Siberia, but nearer to Moscow. Therefore we had not purchased the return tickets because we had to be certain we would have the money left first to complete the job, then to buy the tickets!

It was one of the special miracles of faith that we were prepared to work all the time in Siberia with no guarantee of returning! The whole question of financing the operation when we had not raised even half of the original budget was something which I kept between myself and the Lord. God had promised from the beginning that He would provide the men, the money and the materials and I believed Him, so throughout the whole of the Siberian operation God gave me the faith to not only believe, but act according to that faith.

Publicly in Magadan I had said that my heart was with them and that if I had no tickets to return, I would stay, but I did ask Oleg to order and pay for the tickets to get us at least from Magadan to Khabarovsk on the Sunday night on our way to the next Crusade.

After the final meeting Svetlana and I went with Katie to have supper at the Pastor's apartment before being taken to the airport. It was the Pastor who broke the news saying that Oleg had bought the tickets and had them in his pocket during the meeting along with the passports for the whole of our group. With such a troubled look he told us that the tickets had been stolen out of Oleg's pocket. I asked for more information, especially as to whether the passports had been stolen at the same time, as this would prevent us buying replacements. He unfortunately did not know. We would have to wait until Oleg came later and ask him.

We rejoined the rest of the group after supper and finished packing ready to leave, but shared the problem with the central and ground teams. We did pray over the problem, but felt that God would undertake. God had worked so many miracles already, surely this was not beyond His power to resolve!

Oleg came. Was God taking us at our word and ensuring that we would stay in this place of destiny or not? All we could do, Oleg said, was go to the airport. They might issue new tickets if a record had been kept. But we would need proof of identity. Had our passports been stolen too? Unable to contain himself any longer, Oleg laughed and laughed. He admitted he had decided, together with the Pastor to pay me back for all my jokes and play the biggest practical joke of all on us!

Chapter 19

KRASNOKAMENSK - MISHA
RESCUES US

The first leg of our journey to the next Crusade was the 1.40 am flight which would take us out of Magadan. I had many regrets at leaving here, the farthest point East in our itinerary. The Lord had spoken to me so strongly about this point, that the awakening for the whole of the Russias would begin in the East. This was the focal point of so many prophecies, both recent and historic. But was this the place, or was there another? Was this the time, or must I wait just a little longer? Only God knows this, but for us, once on our way we would slowly retrace our route back westwards and towards home. If I go I must come back. I believe with all my heart what God has promised, He never fails. I make a commitment, I will come back, I will keep hold of God until He answers and fulfils the vision completely.

Arriving at our first stop, Khabarovsk, for the seventh and last time, at 3.00 am local time, it was a relief to see our friend Pastor Yuri and the new car we had bought for him. He offered to take all of us to a small apartment where the eleven of us although cramped for space, could at least rest until our flight to Irkutsk at 11.00 am.

The only thing was to accept Pastor Yuri's hospitality and so we were taken to the apartment, which we reached at 4.00 am. There we found two rooms in which the eleven of us could rest for a couple of hours. Although it was empty because the family were away, a church member from the adjoining apartment came in and spent the next two hours preparing a wonderful breakfast of 'borsch' (soup), potatoes, salad, bread, pancakes, tea and coffee. The problem was that like most of the group, I was too tired to eat much at that unearthly hour!

Eventually we returned to the airport for the next flight which left for Irkutsk at 11.00 am, arriving there at 3.00 pm. Now we had another problem. Although we had been told we would be met, no one was waiting to give us information regarding the tickets which we had assumed had been reserved for the next flight into Chita. I had been booked for a TV interview next morning in Chita. Would I make it in time?

Although there were still three flights operating into Chita that day, there were no seats left for us. We tried desperately to secure cancellations, but despite promises that we would eventually make it, none were available. The Crusade beginning next day was now the priority, so I took the only way out and managed to charter an AN 26 for the next morning, the cargo version of our favourite AN 24, in which we had flown so many thousands of miles. Unfortunately we would have to stay another night at the airport. This was our fifth time to pass through Irkutsk, and I knew that the airport hotel was situated just a few hundred yards from the terminal, so we did not have far to go.

The sombre dilapidated building now used as an airport hotel must have been quite elegant at some time in its history, probably before conversion to a hotel. The staircase was impressive, as were some of the ornate cornices in the large rooms. Now they were just uncomfortable, bare rooms with no facilities except the six beds ranged round the walls. What were supposed to be the bathrooms were appalling, just one filthy room for the men and another for the women on each floor, serving up to forty rooms.

There was no hot water and only two basins, the toilets were typical 'Russian type', with no seats and apparently never cleaned and it was as well that we always carried our own toilet paper, as none was available.

As usual there was no restaurant and nowhere to get anything to eat or drink in the building. We had stayed here once before, so knew that we just had to make the most of it. With all the equipment we were carrying and the need to check in for the charter flight before 7.30 am next day, we did not want to go any further, it would have meant hiring transport and travelling at least a thirty minute drive into the town. Which reminds me, I cannot remember ever seeing this town although we have been through the airport five times in all.

We did manage to find some food in the airport - Russian style hot dogs, but at least it was better than nothing for the hungry group. Rick still had his heating element, so afterwards we went and sat in the room he shared in the hotel, while he made us all some sweet Russian tea. In the early days, Rick had even managed to find us some biscuits or something to have with the tea. By now even Rick's seemingly inexhaustible supply had dried up, so we just had the tea on its own.

I urgently needed to phone the EuroVision office in England, it had been very difficult to maintain communication with them throughout the long weeks I had been away and I urgently needed information. So as Svetlana was exhausted, I took one of the Ukrainians, Yura, who was doing such an excellent job helping with the sound system. Together, he and I and some of the others who felt like a walk went back to the airport buildings, where I knew there was a Post Office from which I could at last make the call back to my office in England. All I had to do was book the call, then wait an hour or so for it to come through. I was very tired and hoped that there would be no big queue or extra delay as all I wanted to do was get some rest.

After dragging myself wearily back again to the airport terminal I found there was a notice stuck on the kiosk window saying that the only woman on duty had gone for supper and there would be an hour's wait before the telephone office would even re-open. I could not face what would now be a minimum of a two hour wait. Although it was only lunch time in England it was already 10.00 pm here in Irkutsk. But remember that I had been travelling most of the previous night and had only slept for two hours at the most. I went disconsolately back to the hotel hoping that the office, and my wife back in England, could understand how difficult it was to make phone calls from Siberia.

Seven thirty next morning found us struggling to carry all the equipment back across the road from the hotel to the terminal. There had been no possibility of finding any breakfast in the hotel, just the luxury of a welcome glass of Rick's tea, which we all desperately needed after waking early to wash and dress as best we could in the discomfort of this filthy hotel.

We waited interminably in the Intourist section of the airport building for information about the charter flight. Despite all my requests, we could get no details of when we should commence to check-in. All that they could tell us was that they would announce when the plane would be ready. By 9.00 am when I had still received no news, I was becoming worried, especially as I had been forced to pay for the charter the night before. Despite my reservations about doing so they had said that without payment in advance they could not guarantee the departure of the aircraft early in the morning as I had requested.

Now all they would give me were various unlikely excuses such as that there was bad weather at our destination, Krasnokamensk, or that the plane was waiting to be refuelled, or that there were problems with our payment of an airport tax, but still no news of our flight departure. So it was with great relief that after having gone to every person I could find, eventually at about 10.00 they called us to go through that awful, wearying process which they call check-in. Weigh everything twice, put it all through the X-ray scanner, the sound system, amplifiers, as well as baggage, then find where they have hidden the transfer bus, persuade them to move it nearer to the door in order to shorten the distance we have to carry all two tons of equipment and baggage. After all this it was a relief that we had chartered an AN 26, which is the freight version of the aircraft, and we have a rear loading ramp and can easily carry everything off the bus and on board ready for departure.

I waited anxiously for the big, powerful, turbo charged engines to burst into life, then watched through the windows while these, first one then the other almost throbbing with the same anxiety, spun the slow moving propellers into a frenzy of activity. At last the pilots could move the airplane into position for take-off and the three hour flight.

As the small airfield at Krasnokamensk came into view through the side windows, the big noisy machine dropped down lower. Still suspended by its high wings, it then lost speed as the pilots reduced the power of the engines until it settled with a groan of protest from its landing gear onto the runway. As the pilots finally switched off the noisy engines and opened the cabin door, we were greeted by a sudden welcome to this new world of total silence. At first the airfield seemed to be totally deserted, until the absolute calm was broken by the arrival of the airport staff who needed some papers and more money for the final payment from me. I climbed down the ramp with the others to be met by the local Pastor and Richard, leader of the ground team.

I was last to leave the airport. Because I still had to pay the final part of the charter cost, the others had unloaded everything into the waiting vehicles before I was ready. I never discovered why, but when chartering these Russian aircraft we always paid part of the money in advance, then the last part had to be paid after we landed. This was the cost of the amount of 'avgas' (the fuel these machines used) it took to refuel the aircraft, and this could only be calculated after we landed. Even when we put down half-way to refuel, I still had to pay this cost at that point, although the price was always calculated in advance! It seemed as if Aeroflot had no credit system to buy the fuel even with its own airports, everything was in cash!

Before leaving the airport I tried in vain to discover if we would be able to get a flight out of here after the service on Wednesday night. Misha had warned us that we needed to be in Chita by 8.00 am Thursday or we would not be able to connect with the scheduled flight for which he had booked us tickets. This was the only one which would enable us to arrive in time for our final Crusade in Bratsk. The airport at Krasnokamensk was very small, there were very few flights to anywhere! Certainly there were no airplanes to charter. We would need to leave immediately after the service on the Wednesday, but how? There were no available airplanes!

It was good to be able to relax for a couple of hours and prepare for the opening meeting of this Crusade. The accommodation was pleasant, it was always better to stay with members of the local church in their own apartments, than to have the dormitory style accommodation in so called hotels. It was difficult enough for me to get time with the Lord, in preparation, because of the very hectic itinerary, but this became almost impossible if I had to share a room with three or four others. Also these warm and friendly believers prepared wonderful meals for us, which saved a lot of time. So often in the hostels we missed meals altogether, unless we had sufficient time to go shopping and buy food. There are not many restaurants or cafes in these towns. Sometimes just none at all. Many times if it was possible, we ate meals with the ground teams. They were in a better position than us because they had already spent a week in the place and had a large enough group to be able to appoint one or two members to deal with the shopping and cooking.

The couple with whom I was staying had their own car, so they were able to take me quickly down to the stadium in time for the meeting. This was only a small town, but already the seats were crowded in anticipation. They were not to be disappointed, again the power of God fell upon the meeting. Unfortunately the sound system was not at its best. By now the loudspeakers which we had brought were becoming badly damaged with the constant travel, but despite this the music group were wonderful, bringing such a sense of the Lord's presence. It was not difficult to minister and the response from the crowds demonstrated this. It was exciting again to see virtually every unbeliever respond to the call when I invited them to come forward, so that over two thousand received Christ. Then together with the Pastor I counselled and prayed with them and prepared them for the follow-up programme which would bring them into the local church.

As the music group ministered again, I called all the sick and crippled to come forward for prayer. Praying for them collectively, many were healed, but the real miracles seemed to happen when I went amongst them and with feeling and compassion began to pray for them individually.

One of the first to be brought through the crowd of many hundreds was an old woman, paralysed on her left side and in great pain, she was instantly set free. When the people see the first miracle, it releases the faith in the others to believe. The next was one of the many babushkas; she hobbled forward with her stick, pain in her body and in her eyes. She had arthritis in her leg and hip, but immediately as I called on the Lord, she was set free, just like the deaf and dumb girl who followed. One after the other, the sick were healed. Seven young girls, a boy and a babushka, all with bad sight, were healed by God's power. So many others were healed of arthritis, spinal problems and deafness.

Next morning I called the central team together for intercession, reminding them that although this was almost the end of this big Siberian Crusade, it was not the end but the beginning. After this the Pastor took us for a barbecue lunch by the river on the Chinese border. There were some fishermen there who recognised me from the posters and advertising which had covered this small town. It was fascinating to be so close to China. The fishermen had a small inflatable boat and offered to take us over the short stretch of water. I had stood at the Chinese border before, at Blagoveshchensk, and prayed over that nation. God had made it quite clear to me that my call and vision are for Russia, then down into the rest of Europe. Others must concentrate on China. I see Russia so strongly both in individual and scriptural prophecy and must not either dilute this vision or go outside God's call on my life. So I looked at China and prayed for the salvation of the nation, but turned back to my first love, Russia.

After the miracles of last night the crowds in the small football stadium had almost doubled for this final meeting. Many were stood on the grass as the praise team ministered both in testimony and song, with great power. Speaking was so easy. I said, ''Today is the day for God to bless Russia. There is an open door, a new freedom that you haven't had for more than seventy years to preach the Gospel about Jesus Christ, and we want to do it now while we have the chance.''

We saw the same blessing as last night, with every unsaved person streaming forward onto the field. The fact that almost 3,000 of them came forward in one night alone in this small town was going to change the whole area and demonstrate who Jesus is. Even if some go back to their old ways and do not remain faithful to Christ, just as Jesus demonstrated with the parable of the sower, at least they have both heard and seen the glory of God. The final outcome is between them and the Holy Spirit. What God wants to do is to demonstrate His power and glorify the Name of Jesus. The Bible does not say that all the world will be saved but that 'the whole earth shall be filled with the glory of God,' Numbers 14:21. This will happen when we, under the power and anointing of the Spirit, glorify Christ before the people, by preaching and healing the sick in His Name. This was the command of Christ Himself in both Luke 9 and 10, when He called the disciples to preach the Gospel and heal the sick.

I began to follow the ministry by calling forward the sick for prayer. Tonight time would be limited because we had to leave by 8.30 pm. Misha had arranged for a charter flight to come in and rescue us. Despite the shortness of time and the fact that my faithful scribe had other duties, arranging for our speedy departure, I saw some outstanding miracles which I was able to record later, like the two young girls whose mothers testified that they were both healed of curvature of the spine. With a great crowd of many hundreds pressing forward for healing, especially as faith had risen following last night's miracles, people were healed one after the other, many with blindness and eye problems, also a boy who was both deaf and dumb and a man delivered from heart trouble. It was not easy for me to break away and leave the sick. I love to bring them healing in Jesus' Name and demonstrate His glory, but I was able to leave the members of the ground team, Team A, under the leadership of Richard Wood still praying as I climbed into the Pastor's car and set off for the small airfield, as fast as possible.

Already the sun was sinking in the west, creating its own sense of urgency. We had been warned that there were no landing lights at this airfield, so the incoming aircraft had to both land and take off again before the light faded. This would put a lot of responsibility on the pilot because, even now, we had stretched the time to its limits. Would everyone in the group who had gone on first with the baggage, be on board waiting for Svetlana and me to come last? Would the pilot, anxious to take off in the fading light leave without me? Were the landing lights operational at Chita? I knew that the runway reconstruction was not yet finished and that we had experienced problems with late night landings at Chita before.

All these questions filled my mind as the Pastor drove furiously the few miles to where we hoped that the plane would still be waiting for us. Even the message confirming that Misha had arranged a charter aircraft to rescue us had come through one of the team members whose English was somewhat limited.

The sight of the big AN 24 on the ground was a wonderful relief and a real answer to prayer. But to my delight, as we drove onto the field and right up to the airplane, who should come out of the door but Misha himself! Smiling and obviously enjoying himself, he had not only rescued us, but as I looked around, our team along with some of the church members from Chita were busy unloading about two tons of the New Testaments which we had brought up to Siberia for the new converts. Misha had brought them over to give to the Pastor here in Krasnokamensk, so that every one of those new believers would have the Word of God in their hands!

The light had faded by the time all the New Testaments were unloaded and all our equipment and baggage put on board. However these pilots are Russians, they did not hesitate, although we prayed fervently as the lumbering machine slowly taxied to the end of the landing strip. Waving our last good-byes to the Pastor and our new friends through the windows illuminated by the cabin lights, we felt the speed increase as the engines reached maximum power. The bumping ceased and I knew that God had worked another miracle, we were airborne, as if carried on angels' wings.

I was still able to make out some of the landscape as we flew for an hour and a half, nearly two hours towards Chita. Rising steadily upward as the powerful twin turbo motors cut through the still night air, the light increased. Down below the ground became shrouded with a blanket of darkness, broken only by the occasional twinkling lights of some of the buildings in the villages and outposts we passed over. Up here as we floated in the air the sun still lingered for a few minutes longer, colouring the sky with beautiful hues of orange turning to red until it finally sank out of sight. Now we were alone in this man-made machine, suspended between heaven and earth, a group of Spirit filled believers, rejoicing in the glory of our God and the fact that we were doing His bidding, preaching the Gospel, healing the sick in obedience to His call. I felt such a peace and joy flooding not just my soul but my whole being. He had called me to Siberia, promising that He would give me the men, the money and the materials. So many had doubted that such a mission could ever be fulfilled. Many thought that either the money would run out, or I would not be able to stand the strain of such an intense itinerary, preaching and travelling without a break for nine weeks in the difficult conditions of Siberia.

But I was glorifying God, here I was, on my way to Bratsk, only one more Crusade and the whole adventure would be complete, every promise from God fulfilled. I had known from the beginning that He who calls us will fulfil the calling, despite all the attacks which come against us, and the onslaught of the devil unleashed against us in his fury. Nothing would stop me and I rejoiced all the more as I saw in the distance the lights of the town of Chita appearing below, and this big, God-directed machine began its slow descent from the realms of glory into the reality of a world suffering under Satan's attack. I stepped out of that aircraft in the power of the Holy Spirit. Like my namesake of old, David, I will not rest until Satan is defeated, his power broken and men set free from the chains of sin and sickness. Christ has all power and all authority, and He has given this to me, so that I can and will conquer in His Name.

Chapter 20

BRATSK - ONLY THE BEGINNING OF THE END

I spent the night in an apartment belonging to one of the members of the church here in Chita. Getting up soon after 6.00 am, I left the comfort of this place which was already familiar as I had stayed here several times before, to be in the airport early to check-in for the 8.00 am flight to Bratsk. Unfortunately the Zavtra spirit took control again resulting in several delays, so that the scheduled flight did not finally depart until 4.00 pm. By the time we eventually arrived at the airport in Bratsk the weather had changed, reminding us that the short Siberian summer was fast giving place to the severity of the coming winter. The rain just poured out of the heavily laden clouds.

Our accommodation was with the rest of the ground team in a large hostel block. Most of the rooms were for two or four but I was given a room to myself which had its own bathroom. Well, there was a small en-suite room with a wash basin, toilet - this time actually with a seat - and what was supposed to be a shower. This appliance was broken, but the previous occupant had managed with the aid of a piece of plastic hose pipe supported on the wall, to rig up a supply of water from the taps of the wash basin. If I stood under this Heath Robinson contraption, water actually came out on top of me, so I suppose it could be designated as a shower. Cold shower of course, hot water not being available. As most of the others had nothing except a communal shower room somewhere in a maze of the corridors and connecting rooms, this was a major blessing for me. Our meals were served in one of the Church member's apartments, this meant either a twenty minute walk or a journey of about three stops on the crowded local bus. As most of the time it was wet and only occasionally did the Pastor collect me, I usually went on the bus.

It was good to have fellowship with the groups here. This was truly the beginning of the end of this first part of the Siberian Adventure. I took advantage of the opportunity to call the whole group together so that I could not only remind them of why we had come here, but also show that we would return next year.

This was also the beginning of the end of the summer period which had allowed us to hold meetings in the open air. It seemed as if the Siberian winter that had held off for so long was drawing near at last. For all these past nine weeks I had heard of the severity of the cold and the extreme conditions which would hold this whole region in its grip. Even though the town in which this Crusade was being held was not in the north, being situated on the near side of Lake Baikal, and our furthest point west, the cold and wet conditions which would herald the onset of the frost and snows of winter, had already begun.

The pouring rain which had continued relentlessly and threateningly prevented us using the stadium for our opening meeting. This was only the second time that the weather had succeeded in causing this to happen in the ten weeks the teams had been in Siberia. The other occasion being the opening night in Magadan. We had no choice but to hold the meeting in a sports hall under the actual stadium. Not so many attended, but over 200 decided for Christ, remarkable considering the circumstances. We also had a tremendous number of healings. Katie recorded more than twenty-five outstanding miracles. As the rain continued unabated, the Saturday meeting was transferred to a cinema.

Numbers attending were about the same, but this time 300 accepted Christ. A choir of young people from a local church sang with such sadness, afraid to smile. (However when the meeting was over they asked our praise and worship team to teach them both how to sing our lively songs and also how to smile and to express their joy in Christ.)

After the worship I prayed for the people, ''Father bless this town. Father we want You to take away the sadness from Russia and bring new blessing and joy and happiness. I pray this town will find the joy of really knowing Jesus Christ.'' Now I began to preach:

> God wants to bring a new blessing and spiritual awakening that will change Russia. You are in a window of time - you have come out of one period of trouble and you are about to go into another period of trouble and difficulty - but in this moment of time now, God is going to visit Russia and He will change the face of the whole of your nation. This is a tremendous miracle.

> You see, God loves Russia, He wants to reach out and bless you as never before and I want to show you how. I have been able to love and serve the Lord since I was eight years old, and I have seen how God changes people's lives. Jesus Christ is alive today. There is no other help for Russia. Yeltsin won't help Russia, Zhirinovsky won't help Russia. Zhirinovsky was in Magadan and held a political rally there before our crusade. He didn't preach the Gospel that we did. He preached war and death and a lot of other things.

> Why do I heal the sick? All I want to do is introduce you to Jesus. Jesus is coming back! And the Bible says when He comes everybody will see Him, everybody in Russia,

everybody all over the world. I'm going to see the Jesus I love who healed my cancer and forgave my sin! He's coming soon - but He's only coming for those who love Him.

If you don't receive forgiveness for your sins, you'll spend eternity with the Stalins and Zhirinovskys. (Now that makes you laugh!) Or do you want to spend eternity with Jesus? How? Believe in a miracle that Jesus is alive, that He died to forgive your sins. I've waited thirty years to come to Bratsk to tell you how much Jesus loves you and how much He wants you to love Him.

That night the emphasis in healing seemed to be on the eyes. Seven people at least were healed of either blindness or very poor sight, and I was particularly touched the way one satisfied old man firmly put his glasses away in his jacket. He didn't need them now! At the end a young woman, a member of our ground team here, a girl I had seen grow up from childhood in my own town, came up to me. "David," she said, "you never knew, but I have been blind from birth in my right eye. The optical nerve was never connected to the brain, but tonight, if you pray, I have faith." It was no problem to God. She was instantly healed! Even the optical nerve was rejoined.

Next morning, Sunday, I had the choice of speaking at a lively local charismatic church, or travelling to another some distance away which was very traditional and dead. I chose the latter, feeling that they needed the message most. I said,

I believe in the Fire and Power of God. I have a burden for your nation - God is speaking to Russia today more than any other nation of the world. God is wanting to pour out His Spirit on Russia. I want to call down and to see the

Power and Glory of God. I believe in miracles, in the Power of God, I see the Power of God. I am so excited by what God is doing in your nation. We'll see hundreds of thousands come into the Kingdom, saved from hell and brought into Christ.

I'm going to work here till everyone of you is on fire for God. Since we've been here in Siberia we've probably seen 1000 people miraculously healed. There is nothing God can't do! The only way to get this experience is found in Acts 1:8, through the Power of the Holy Ghost. If you get filled with the Power of God, fire will come into your soul, your bones. "You will receive power after that the Holy Ghost comes on you and you will be witnesses to Me in Jerusalem, in Judea, in Samaria and to the ends of the earth."

That's what Jesus said to the early Church! What happened when the Fire fell? Fire burned in them! We need the Fire of God in Russia! Are you hungry for God? Look what happened to those early disciples; they'd experienced the greatest miracle on earth - for three years they'd lived with Jesus. After three days in the grave the Spirit of God came into the body of Jesus, and when the Power came, the stone rolled away and Jesus came out alive! We should be so thrilled, so excited!

What happened to the early Church? They'd seen Jesus live and die, they'd seen the resurrection - but they went into an upper room, locked the door, put bars on the windows and for fifty days they were afraid of the secret police! I don't see any record of anyone getting saved or healed. They were sad until Pentecost came.

Then the Fire came down and the Power burned in them, and on that day they broke down the doors, climbed up on the roof and, in the Power of the Holy Ghost, preached the Gospel in the language of everyone that heard them. On that day God saved 3000 men. That is the Power of God.

In these last days, God will pour out a greater outpouring! God's put a burning vision in my heart. He has chosen the nation of Russia that's seen more suffering and persecution than any other nation in the world. God wants to stir up your nation and your people. Jesus is coming back! Why does God want to pour out another Pentecost? Why are your people standing around doing nothing ... Jesus is coming again!

When Jesus was on the earth 2000 years ago, nobody knew Him. He began preaching and healing the sick. He called first twelve and then seventy-two and told them, "Go in My Name, preach the Gospel, heal the sick, raise the dead. Stir the people up, get men on fire, so that when I come they'll know who I am. Give the people joy, happiness, take away their sin, their sickness, their pain, their suffering." That's what Jesus said! "Before I come preach the Gospel, heal the sick, work the miracles." Jesus is coming back! Do you really believe the Bible? - You don't!

Jesus is coming back, but in Russia they don't know who He is and that God loves them. If Jesus came back tomorrow, they wouldn't know Him. Jesus says to you, 'Before I come, I want you to go to every town, every village, every apartment block, and, because they won't believe you, heal the sick.'

Have you done it? NIET! No! Why are there empty places in your church? There should be 100,000 people here today! The people in Bratsk want to know God. In the pouring rain on Friday 400 people came willing to stand in a wet stadium because they are so hungry to know God. They're YOUR neighbours, YOUR people, hungry for God. How many hours do you preach the Gospel? How many did you save this week? How many did you heal? You say, I can't preach the Gospel, but Jesus says, when the Holy Spirit comes, you'll receive power to preach the Gospel. Mark 16 says those who believe will drive out demons, they'll speak in new tongues and they'll lay their hands on the sick and they will recover. You need the Power of God.

Revival can come to your town in a day. God can do it if we will cry out to Him. Nothing is impossible. When your Church is on fire with the Power of the Holy Ghost you won't have empty seats. When you fast and pray, when you call on God, when you go out on the streets then your church will be filled.

"Our street evangelists are going home today. They've seen as many as fifty people receive Jesus in one meeting on the streets. The people of Bratsk are hungry to receive Jesus and YOU are the only ones who can reach them. When you go to fast and pray next week, you will receive power and you will be witnesses. I'm going home tomorrow. I'm leaving you to carry on the work I've started, God is putting this responsibility on YOU. God has promised me He'd raise up Evangelists and Pastors so that the work I've begun won't stop but carry on."

When I finished speaking there was a silence, broken as one

after the other these people responded, crying out to God in prayer, to receive this same anointing that they might respond in the power of the Holy Spirit.

By the Sunday evening the Lord had answered prayer and the rain had stopped, though the weather was becoming very cold, so we held the service in the same cinema as the previous night. The cinema was packed to capacity and nearly 700 came forward to accept Christ. Despite the weather, in the three days we had been in Bratsk, more than 1200 responded to the Gospel invitation, prayed with me and were counselled by our teams. The sick who came forward in their hundreds at this last meeting were wonderfully healed as confirmation of God's power.

At supper afterwards the assistant Pastor shared with us how a wonderful thing had happened prior to the Crusade. When he, with Pastor Peter and his wife had been in prayer about the coming evangelisation, a woman had come to them to tell them of a vision she had received from the Lord. While in prayer she had seen a large harvest field being cut by a combine harvester and afterwards women were gathering the remains of the harvest. The assistant Pastor said to me, "Brother, the first part of the vision has been fulfilled!" I think this church will fulfil the second part!

On the way to the airport in Pastor Peter's car on the Monday, he gave us confirmation of the demonstration of God's power. The city of Bratsk is in two parts, both with the same name, but separated by about thirty miles on either side of a massive dam. The Friday night meeting had been in the other part of the city where his father was Pastor and they had been saddened at the appalling weather. On the Sunday morning however, how delighted they were when the people who had attended on the Friday night came again and brought all their friends! The church was packed and the power of God came down. Miracles of healing which had begun on the Friday, continued. The blind and the deaf were healed. He urgently asked us to come back next year, but to stay not for three days, but at least four to five days. And please to come in the better weather!

It being the end of a great summer campaign, Misha had come all the way from Chita to visit me on the Sunday, staying overnight and sharing my room in the hotel. With Svieta's help we had sorted out all the remaining administrative details and with God's help, found enough money to pay all the bills. Now we began to rejoice in all that the Lord had accomplished during these past weeks and to look forward to next year.

Again I repeated the question which I had asked earlier, "Misha, do you still love me?" There was no hesitation in his positive reply. Then he began to outline a bigger and more successful operation which he proposed for next year.

Chapter 21

AND THE MIRACLES WENT ON
AND ON...

We had promised our Ukrainian brethren a year ago that we would work with them and hold several Crusades in the Ukraine following the big programme in Siberia. So after a brief interlude of just two weeks in the office in England to enable us to prepare, we were on our way. The miracles which had so marked the fulfilment of God's promises in Siberia did not cease but rather increased, not only, as we were to see and experience, in the healings, but also in all the other miracles in the natural realm which had so marked the confirmation of God on the ministry during the summer.

This time I was not flying, but travelling by car. This was the only way to cover the great distances between the crusades and also transport the new loudspeaker equipment from England. We had made the decision to leave the original heavy loudspeakers in Chita with Misha, though the other parts of the system had been brought back into the Ukraine and would be waiting for us.

Everything was fine, we travelled easily across Europe and into Poland in the big Volvo Estate. The car ran well although the equipment was extremely heavy and the car, being overloaded, was sitting low on the road. With a right hand drive western car we saved a lot of time at the border between Poland and the Ukraine, by driving past the waiting Ukrainians and going direct to the border. We were used to doing this as sometimes the Eastern nationalities wait not hours but days for their permission to cross, whereas we could get through quickly if we acted boldly.

At first things were normal on the run down the Ukrainian roads. Through years of travel in these parts I am used to the potholes, rough broken surfaces, and slow moving, grossly overloaded trucks which shed bits of anything from timber to potatoes directly in front of you. As we left Kiev behind us in the early evening, facing the prospect of another night drive for the final 500 miles into Lughansk things were still under control. My real concern was for fuel supplies. Petrol was very difficult to obtain and the heavily laden car, travelling very fast, was rather thirsty. Most of the few filling stations situated up to 100 miles apart had no fuel at all. We had to rely on either a (stolen ?) petrol tanker sitting just off the road with a hand-written sign saying 92 or 76 which was the octane rating of the petrol he was selling for up to double the normal price, or one of the private cars stopped on the verge, with dirty twenty-litre containers waiting for a desperate motorist who, running out of petrol, would pay anything, usually in dollars for a very dubious mixture supposedly of petrol.

It was now very dark and the roads becoming more difficult, no proper surfaces, part dual carriageways suddenly changing either into single without warning, or worse, switching into either lane without notice because of road works. This meant that you could not tell in the dark who or what was coming next. A further complication was the general refusal of the drivers to put on their lights, some travelling with no lights at all or only on parking lights. Cyclists, tractors and other varieties of vehicle invariably had nothing to warn you either of their presence, or the fact that the slow moving vehicle you were about to pass would swerve suddenly in front of you to overtake, or perhaps to dodge a worse than usual pothole which had appeared mysteriously in front of them as if from deep below the ground.

Passing yet another of the broken down vehicles littering the edge of the road - mechanical failure or more likely burst tyres - I turned to my navigator, who had a God given gift to understand not only our map but also to translate the Cyrillic script of the road signs which confusingly varied between the Russian and Ukrainian language, and said "What a terrible place this would be to break down." Almost as if the devil was listening, within minutes I both heard and felt the jolt as the car hit something. Although travelling at about 60 mph, and conscious that the front tyre was burst, I brought the car to a stop as swiftly as I could.

It was the worst possible situation, a burst front tyre, no way I could bring the car further off the road, very dark, and these noisy but almost invisible monsters passing ominously close. To get to the spare wheel and tools meant unloading onto the dust and dirt of the roadside all the loudspeakers, stands, microphones, cables and other impedimenta loaded so carefully in daylight at our office some days ago. Our only security from the passing vehicles was the emphasis Volvo have on safety which meant that our car was surrounded by brilliant flashing lights, and the ring of angels which we prayed that the Lord would send to protect us in such a vulnerable position.

It took an hour before the job was finished and the equipment re-loaded. Cleaning ourselves up we gave thanks to the Lord and attempted to re-commence our journey. Feeling the vibration as I moved off, my instinctive reaction was that the impact had damaged either the brakes or steering. This time pulling slowly into a more secure position on the roadside I quickly found that the problem was that the impact of hitting the oversized pothole in the over loaded car had not only badly damaged the front but also the rear wheel. Only now was I fully aware of the gravity of the situation.

Two wheels were badly damaged, not just the tyres, but the

whole rims of front and rear wheels were so bad that the edge of one rim was split off from the centre, and the other pushed in at three points so that even supposing the tyre could be repaired, it would not hold air pressure. Even with an inner tube the car could not be driven. The only spare was now on the front, but the car could not be driven or even towed without at least one new wheel and tyre. Of course being a Volvo, I quickly realised no Russian cars had wheels remotely able to fit. Now 9.00 at night, we were stranded 100 miles east of Kiev, no civilisation near, no village or habitation visible in the dark, no telephones, 400 miles from the Crusade which begins tomorrow, our interpreter Svieta gone on in front of us with the bus group and already relaxing in Lughansk, no rescue service for us and no roadside help in the Ukraine. In the ten hours we were to spend there no one stopped. If only the police would come now!

We spent the hours of darkness alternating between prayer and a practical realisation that in the natural help would not come. Unlike a western country where eventually some friendly person would come along, here with an inability to communicate we had to first assess the situation accurately and secondly be in a position that when daylight came we could begin to do something positive. But what?

As daylight broke I saw the car stop briefly on the other side of the road. Did I really see the flash of an angel's wings as I strained my sleepy tired eyes, did I see the fire and smoke as the 'chariot' stopped? I wish ... I wish ... all I know is that, at this first sign of help, I leapt out and ran across the road. The driver did not speak English and my few words were not suitable for the occasion, but when I brought him over and in the first pale light of the new day he saw the situation, his reaction was swift and miraculous. Lifting out his spare wheel, I recognised that this Ukrainian was driving of all things a large German Opel Omega, that his wheels were the same size as mine, and that he was going to jack up my car for me and fit his own wheel! Then he motioned me to wait with his companion, said recognisably, ''Police'' and drove off quickly. Returning five minutes later he motioned to me to follow him in my now drivable car with the damaged wheel on the roof. Two miles down the road he turned into a lane, at the bottom of which to my indescribable amazement, was a fully equipped car repair depot with its own special tyre bay! He indicated by writing in the dust on my rear window that the men would come to work at 8.00 am, took back his own wheel leaving my car perched on its jack, then before leaving put his hand in his pocket and took out two paper notes each 100,000 coupons and vanished. The time was just 6.30 am.

Only thirty minutes later, as if told by an unseen person, two workmen arrived. They took both damaged wheels and succeeded in making one usable wheel and tyre out of the two! By only 8.00 the job was done, the equipment replaced; I offered the men the money he had given me, then with a dawning consciousness of the wonder of another miracle, drove my four wheeled car slowly back down the lane to rejoin the highway. Had he really been an angel? As we reflected, we saw the similarity with the Good Samaritan. This man had given us his own wheel, he took us to the 'Inn' and he had taken out two notes. Ukrainian Angel or Good Samaritan, it was a real miracle, the impossible had happened, and all that we had done was cry out to our Father. Real need, real prayer. And what had we prayed in the desperation of that lonely night? ...... for a special big miracle to demonstrate that the anointing of Siberia was on us in greater measure.

And so this was how the miracles which began in Siberia were continued in the Ukraine. Now we prepare for the next phase when we return to Siberia and the 'Bigger Miracles' begin ......

Chapter 22

THE BEST IS YET TO COME

Between May and October 1994 we held twenty-seven 17-day crusades in Belarus, Siberia and the Ukraine. For me this meant preaching on 5 days out of every 7, travelling enormous distances (approximately 50,000 km altogether), with an army of about 400 co-workers - intercessors, street evangelists, Bible teachers - from the Ukraine, Bulgaria, Czech Republic, Hungary, Germany, Northern Ireland and Britain. We saw approximately 100,000 saved - as many as were saved in the first six months of the 1904 Welsh Revival - and we recorded approximately 1300 miracles of healing in writing as they occurred (not counting those prayed for by my 400 co-workers under the same anointing of God, nor any of the healings that happened in Belarus for which we did not have a scribe). I have no great financial backing, but I believed God; in just five months we completed one of the largest, most intensive and difficult evangelistic missions ever undertaken by a British Mission.

Why did I do it ? I did it for two reasons:

Firstly because in August 1991, only days before the attempted coup against Gorbachev and just months before the Soviet Union ceased to exist as a communist state, I prophesied publicly that Russia was on the edge of a precipice. Today Russia is still on that edge. In a letter dated 4th April 1991 I wrote, ''There is a threat of a tremendous backlash in Eastern Europe to the freedom movement which may result in a greater repression than anything seen under either Stalin or Hitler.'' Nothing since has caused me to change my mind. I believe time is very short, and that God has commanded me not to be a Jonah, not to run away, but to get in there with the Gospel fast, and work while it is still day.

Secondly, I go because God has promised me a greater outpouring of His Spirit here, in Russia, than anywhere else in the world - if we will act now before the Antichrist·arises. There is going to be a tremendous spiritual battle, and it is our job to lift up the Name of Jesus and demonstrate to the world who He is by signs and wonders before He returns.

God showed me this in a vision as I was preaching in Bath in February 1993, a vision so strong that it was as if I was already looking back on its fulfilment. Normally a prophet stands on Sunday and prophesies about Monday, but I was actually standing in Tuesday, looking back on what I could already see accomplished, it was so real to me.

These are the words I spoke that day as I preached on Deuteronomy 4:32:

''Ask now of the days that are past which were before you, since the day that God created man upon the earth and ask from one side of heaven to the other whether there has been any such thing as this great thing is or ever been heard like it.'' Now God is beginning to say something quite strong. God is challenging Moses and He's challenging the people, ''Begin to question, begin to ask, look into the past, look into the whole history of the Church, look right back to the beginning of creation, and ask this one question - whether on earth or in heaven, the earth has ever seen, man has ever seen, you have ever seen what God is about to do.''

Now this gets me excited, because God is saying in the last days, He is saying to the Church today, "I am prepared to do something greater, bigger than anything that has ever been seen in the history of the earth, in the history of the Church - I'm about to do it **NOW**!"

The challenge is, God is about to do the greatest act, the greatest miracle the world has ever seen. He's going to raise up prophets, He's going to raise up men like Elijah - He's going to raise up men with an anointing and a power of the Spirit to do the greater works than Jesus did!

There's going to be an enormous battle taking place in Europe, in Russia, and Satan is going to be defeated, his power is going to be broken! There's going to be a spirit of intercession and prayer and praise come upon the Church - the Church is going to be liberated in praise, but only when it gets on its knees. Then God will move in power and authority.

If you only knew what's about to happen, you would not be falling asleep. God is exciting me because I see in the Word what He's about to do now. The greatest Glory, the greatest Power, the greatest ministry, the greatest miracle ... we're going to see miracles of healing we have never seen in our lives. I'm excited - we're going to be saying exactly what Deuteronomy 4 says, 'Ask of the days that are past,' go back, ask history, go back to the Welsh Revival, to the days of Smith Wigglesworth, George and Stephen Jeffries - I was brought up with that - go back to the beginning of time since the day God created man on the earth, ask every saint and say, "Has God ever done anything such as He's going to do today in the Church?" That's the excitement!

We're living in the last days, the days of the return of Christ, the days when we are going to see revival fire bursting upon the Church, poured on the Church, until the Church is going to be living and vibrant and working and believing and moving into spiritual victory - all in the preparation of the glorious return of Jesus. Those days are going to culminate with the sound like a trumpet, and that sound is going to echo from every building, and that trumpet will herald the return of Christ and suddenly in a blaze of Glory sweeping across the sky from the East to the West Christ is going to come back to the earth and He's going to take control, bind Satan, cast Him into a prison for one thousand years ... I'm prophesying what the prophets have been prophesying for 2000 years, I'm just shouting it out. You see, the people will ask this, "Has there ever been any such thing as this great thing? Has anybody seen or heard anything like it in the history of the earth?" Now that's what I'm believing God is going to do now! Oh hallelujah Church, come on!

This is the Pentecost I was seeking God for when I did the overland trip to Jerusalem all those years ago in 1961. This is the Pentecost I have been seeking across Europe ever since. Saints, it's about to fall, and it's going to fall in Russia. That's why I go! That's why I will go again and again, that's why I will sacrifice my life for it.

FINAL WORD

In the few days I was at home in the office between our Siberian Crusades and our Crusades in the Ukraine, a copy of the European Prayer Link Bulletin was put on my desk. How amazed and encouraged I was when I read the following. It said this:

HUDSON TAYLOR 'SAW' TODAY IN 1855

Hudson Taylor, missionary to China and founder of the first truly inter-denominational foreign mission, the China Inland Mission, was graced by God to 'glimpse' some of today's events 140 years ago! On one of his furloughs to England in 1855, Taylor was preaching when he suddenly stopped. He stood speechless for a time with his eyes closed. When he began to speak again he explained:

I have seen a vision. I saw in this vision a great war that encompasses the world. I saw this war recess and then start again, actually being two wars. After this I saw much unrest and revolts that will affect many nations. I saw in some places spiritual awakenings.

In Russia, I saw there will come a general all-encompassing, national SPIRITUAL AWAKENING so great that there could never be another like it. From Russia, I saw the awakening spread to many European countries. Then I saw an all-out awakening, followed by the coming of Christ.

From an original Russian article titled *Spiritual Revival* published in Finland in 1945, reprinted from *Food for Life International*, 1848 Liverpool Road, Suite 253, Pickering, Ontario, L1V 6M3, Canada. Quoted in *Intercessors for America Newsletter*, Vol.21, No.7/8, also in the *European Prayer Bulletin*, 3rd Quarter 1994.

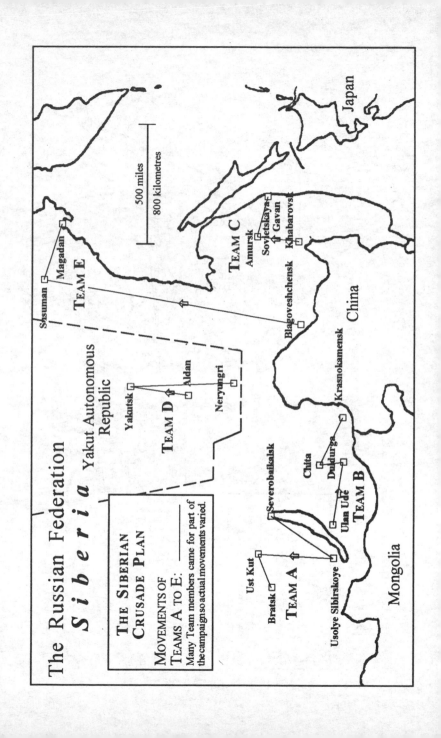

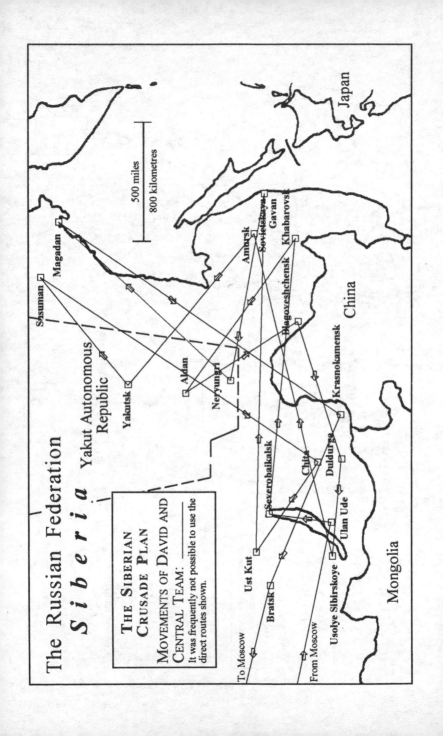

EUROVISION MISSION TO EUROPE

David Hathaway
is still fulfilling God's call
to evangelise and win these
former communist nations to Christ.
Today each crusade is simultaneously broadcast
live on regional TV, reaching 1-3 million with the
Gospel of Jesus Christ every time.
To find out more, or to support this Ministry,
write to:

euro vision
MISSION TO EUROPE

41 Healds Road
Dewsbury
West Yorkshire
WF13 4HU

+44 1924 453693

A Company Limited by Guarantee Registered in England
No. 6638375
Registered Charity no 1126438